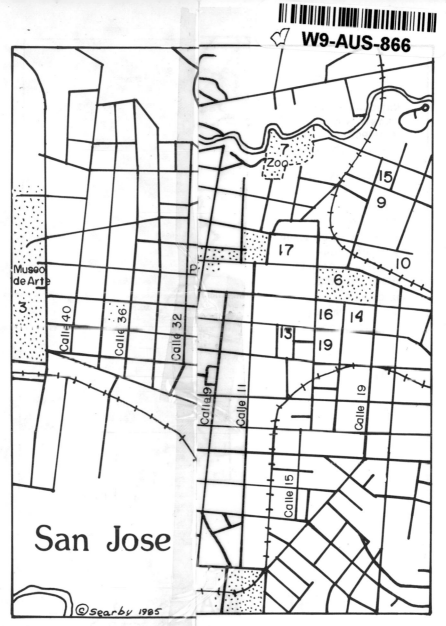

San Jose

©Searby 1985

1 National Theater

2 Plaza de Cultura

3 Sabana Park

4 Parque Central

5 Parque Morazán

6 Parque Nacional

7 National Zoo

8 San Juan de Dios Hospital

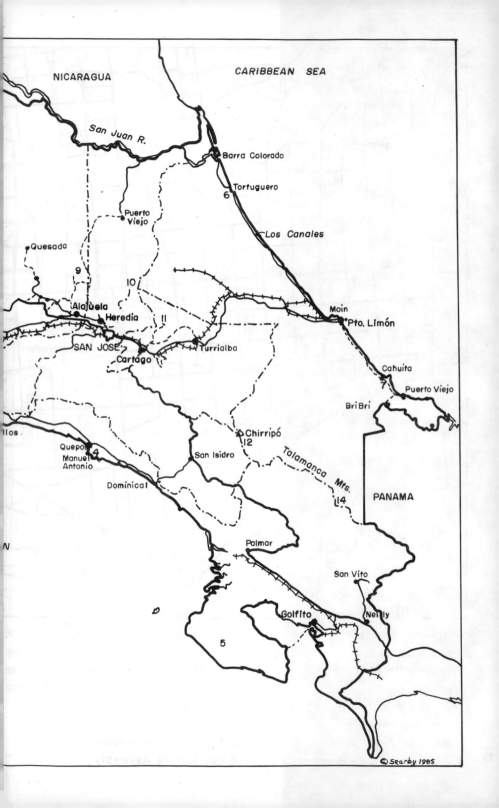

THE
COSTA RICA
TRAVELER

Getting Around
In Costa Rica

By: Ellen Searby

Windham Bay Press
Juneau, Alaska

p. 63, correction in first paragraph:

Any prescription drugs should be in their original containers. If you wear a money belt under clothing, it's wise not to wear it through customs.

Front Cover: Early morning on Third Beach at Manuel Antonio.

Back Cover: An orchid at Cahuita, an iguana at Rincon de la Vieja, and Poás crater.

Windham Bay Press
Box 1332, Juneau, Alaska 99802

FOREWORD

Costa Rica has more choices of things to see and do with less distance between them than any other place I've been. In the space of 75 miles across its narrowest width, the land goes from sea level to over 12,000 feet and back to sea level. There are many landscapes and climates between, and the wide variety of plants and animals they support. Costa Rica would offer fine traveling and vacations even if this were all.

"We have so much to share," is the slogan of Costa Rica's tourism department, the Instituto de Costarricense de Turismo (ICT). Costa Rica has 2½ million of the most friendly, helpful people in the world. A Canadian visitor wrote, "They treat you with a quiet dignity, like a guest in their home, instead of an invading tourist." Their pride in their country, its freedom and literacy, and their willingness to share it with the traveler, are a joy—and a lesson in humanity.

Before I vacationed in Costa Rica the first time, a U.S. friend described it as "the most hassle-free foreign travel you'll ever do." Even with almost no Spanish, except numbers, I found she was right. People helped any time they could think of a way to do so. They've met enough travelers to know what we want and have kept their considerate nature without becoming cynical. Meeting the Costa Ricans is as much a privilege as traveling in the beauty of their country.

Acknowledgments

Many people helped me gather the information in this book, and without them I couldn't possibly have done it. I appreciate their making it an enjoyable and fascinating experience as well. Within the Instituto Costarricense de Turismo (ICT, or Costa Rica Tourist Board) the following people answered hundreds of questions or found someone who could—Edgar Bailey, Laudencio Castro, Robert Chaverri, Elmo Delanoce, Rodrigo Herrera (who drove smoothly over hundreds of miles of primitive roads and trails while explaining his country and people to me), Roberto Morales, Jorge Monge, Francisco Rojas, Arturo Ruiz, Guillermo Sanz, Edwin Salas, and Luis Villavicencio. Costa Rica is lucky, and so are its visitors, to have such dedicated people working for them.

Sra. Maritza Linda helped me through the process of visa extensions and explained it to me for this book. Fabio Carballo gave much practical advice. At Servicio de Parques Nacionales, Fernando Cortez and Cindy Hypke answered questions, gave advice, and made arrangements for me to visit parks. Archie Fields and his staff in San Jose and at Barra Colorado answered questions and introduced me to other useful information sources. Their guides stopped the boat for every bird or monkey I wanted to photograph, and once persuaded some apprehensive and well-armed Nicaraguans on the border that my 210 mm. lens and 3 cameras were for bird pictures. Michael Kaye and Jim Lewis had useful information on access to remote areas and the wildlife found there. And Ken Cameron, long-time host at Rio Colorado Lodge, looked at my Inside Passage guide book and talked this vacationing tourist into doing the research and writing one on Costa Rica.

Any errors in the book are my responsibility, not theirs. They did an incredible job of explaining their country and culture to me. May you enjoy it as much as I do!

Special thanks to Betty Seguin, my assistant, who compiled hotel tables and everything else I could delegate.

TABLE OF CONTENTS

Acknowledgments. 4
Foreword 3
Costa Rica 7
Why Come?   Major Attractions 8
   Beaches 8
   Volcanoes 10
   National Parks 11
   Birds and Wildlife. 13
   Flora 16
   Train to Puerto Limón 18
   "Los Canales"—Inland Waterway 22
   Fishing. 26
   Hunting. 29
   Sports 29
   Theater and Museums 32
Costa Rica —The Nation 36
   Geography and Climate 36
   History 43
   Social Conditions 47
   Agriculture. 49
   Industry. 52
Planning Your Trip 53
   Exchange. 55
   Safety 55
   Cultural Sensitivity 58
   How to Get There (Airlines). 60
   Entry and Departure Requirements 65
   Entering Costa Rica 67
   What to Bring. 68
   Time 70
   Telephones 70
   Addresses 71
   Mail 71
   Getting Around. 73
      Air. 73
      Trains 73
      Buses 73
      Taxis 74
      Car Rental. 77
      Hitchhiking 80

Hotel Comments. 80
Camping 84
Food 85
Health 86
Photography 91
Arts, Crafts, Souvenirs 94
Returning Home—Customs 96
Living in Costa Rica—Pensionados 97
Regions. 105
Meseta Central (including San Jose). 105
East 133
West and Southwest (Puntarenas South) 147
Northwest (including Nicoya Peninsula) 162
North and South Central 186
National Parks (Attractions & Facilities). 188
Sources of Information. 192
Tour Agencies. 192
Embassies & Consultates in/near San Jose. 195
Costa Rican Consulates 196
Recommended Reading. 198
Other Addresses 199
Useful Words and Phrases 201
Flash! As We Go To Press 203
The Author. 205

The Cultural Plaza, National Theater, and the office building which houses ICT. The tourist information desk is under the Cultural Plaza. (ICT)

COSTA RICA

If there is a tropical Camelot, peaceful Costa Rica is it. Despite military and political turbulence in neighbors to the north, Costa Rica has the best working democracy in Latin America, the freest, most honest elections, and the highest literacy rate in the region. Beset with the same economic, social, and environmental problems that face other Third World countries, Costa Rica is much farther along the road to solution than most others.

Costa Rica is tiny, about the size of West Virginia. You can fly into San Jose, the capital, up in the Central Valley, and decide whether you want to swim in the Atlantic or Pacific that afternoon!

7

WHY COME? MAJOR ATTRACTIONS

Costa Rica in its small space has many attractions that are major by any standard. Among them are:

On secluded beach a driftwood bird watches waves by day and nesting leatherback turtles by night.

Beaches

Costa Rica has hundreds of beaches, almost all uncrowded. You may find yourself the only person on a beach five miles long! Do you prefer white, black, yellow, or red sand? Costa Rica has them all. Do you want to surf, snorkel, walk on a wild driftwood-littered beach, watch thousands of sea turtles come ashore to lay eggs in the sand, watch baby turtles freshly hatched crawl down to the sea, swim or wade in calm water, gather agates and moonstones polished by waves, fish for tarpon, marlin, and other gamefish, walk palm-shaded paths along the shore watching for parrots, monkeys, egrets, and end the day enjoying one of the world's finest sunsets?

All Costa Rican beaches seem to have at least four or five of the above features. You can pick an area suited to your interests. Usually several nearby beaches have different attractions, which add variety to your vacation.

Do take seriously local advice on rip currents which exist at most beaches with surf. If you are caught in a current that carries you out, don't exhaust yourself fighting it, but swim parallel to the shore until you are free and then swim back in. Note that you may need to be able to swim for up to an hour—and don't swim in such places unless you can. Study diagrams posted that show you how to recognize and avoid rip currents.

Accommodations vary from some of the world's finest hotels, through very comfortable, reasonably priced cabins and motels, to basic cabinas and rooms, and, of course, camping out. These are described individually in their regions later in this book.

Cahuita's coral beach, part of the national park that includes the only coral reef on Costa Rica's Caribbean coast.

Volcanic ash covers the 11,260-ft. summit of Irazú, a popular day tour from San Jose. On a clear day, usually early, you can see both the Atlantic and Pacific Oceans from its summit.

Volcanoes

Costa Rica's backbone north and east of San Jose is a chain of volcanoes extending down from Mexico through Central America. Costa Rica has 10, 3 of them active. You can ride public buses or bus tours from San Jose to the tops of Irazú, 11,260 ft., and Poás, 9,500 ft. Others are reached by hiking, horse, or jeep trail. Irazú erupted in 1963, showering San Jose with 5 inches of ash, causing millions of colones in damage to property, livestock, and the 1964 coffee crop, but enriching the Central Valley soil for years to come. On a clear morning you can see both the Atlantic and Pacific Oceans from its summit. Poás last erupted in 1978, but has a constantly varying steam cloud boiling up from the fumaroles in its crater. Both volcanoes have overlooks at the edge of their craters with fantastic views of the banded rocks and ash that form their rims. Riding up these heights, you pass from warm to a very cool and cloudy tropical climate. Coffee plantations give way to dairy cattle and potato patches on terraces up the steep slopes. In the cloud forests at higher elevations, tree branches support communities of bromeliads, orchids, and other plants. Up here in the clouds, the forest and the ash-covered slopes near the craters are another world from the busy streets of San Jose.

Park ranger and friend ride past clouds of steam from hot springs in the forest at Rincon de la Vieja.

National Parks

Costa Rica has done an incredible thing for any nation, much less a struggling developing country—it has set aside 8% of its small space in a national park system, one of the world's most important. As tropical forests are cut everywhere, these preserved areas are the only hope of saving many plant and animal species. There is at least one sample of every ecosystem in the country within the park system.

All the volcanic summits are within parks or biological preserves. Santa Rosa is a dry tropical forest, while Corcovado in the southwest is a rolling, wet lowland with as many bird species as the United States and Canada combined. Some parks preserve cultural or archeological features, such as prehistoric village sites.

There's something for most travelers in the parks. You can watch sea turtles come ashore to lay their eggs in the sand at Tortuguero and Santa Rosa and come back several months later to see newly hatched babies scramble down to the sea. At Caño Island and Cahuita you can snorkel on coral reefs. At Rincon de la Vieja you can walk up to thermal springs and "pailes," springs of boiling mud. In Santa Rosa's dry forest, undergrowth and vines are widely spaced and you have clear views of monkeys, coatimundis, peccaries, armadillos, and hundreds of birds. I saw all of these on one walk there.

Costa Rica's limited park budget is going to the preservation of these precious habitats for wildlife, while most unprotected land is being cut over for lumber and to make cattle range. Funds aren't being spent for building plush facilities or even access roads in some cases. While you can drive up to some parks by bus, La Amistad, the newest and largest, covering the Talamanca Range along the Panamanian border, may be "reached" by dirt roads which end 2 days' walk before the park boundaries on both east and west sides. There is not a single lodge or hotel within the parks. For the more remote parks arrangements must be made with park headquarters in San Jose so the staff knows what help you'll need—space in a bunkroom, use of cooking facilities, guide, possibly horses to rent if the rangers don't need them that day, etc.

If your time is limited and you want to see the maximum wildlife in remote parks, you may want to go on a nature tour led by biologists. Smithsonian, the National Audubon Society, Questers, and others organize these. Within Costa Rica there are several outfitters, including **Costa Rica Expeditions**.

Common egret and friend in a Guanacaste pond.

Birds and Wildlife

Costa Rica is home, seasonally, to 1/10th of the world's known bird species, over 850 (the U.S. and Canada combined have about 350)! For such a small country, this seems impossible, but Costa Rica's 12,600 feet of altitude range, wet and dry zones, and strategic location in the overlap between North and South American bird ranges account for it. This nation's dedicated protection of those habitats may be all that keeps many of these species alive.

From trips to the zoo, you know that tropical birds are often brighter and more spectacular than most temperate birds, though nearly invisible types of brown twitters (my term which saves reaching for the bird book) are found in every forest. Chattering groups of parrots and lorikeets fly over many areas in early morning and evening. An early morning look in any hotel garden or city park is rewarding.

13

Costa Rica's pride is the resplendent quetzal, never found in zoos, but living in the high, cool forests of Monteverde and Chirripó. With its red underside, iridescent green back and trailing green tail plumes, it is like no other! It is most easily seen on guided trips in Monteverde in February and March, when it is nesting and less cautious than usual—and the guide knows where the nests are.

Depending on location, season, and luck, you may see scarlet macaws, tanagers and orioles, toucans, waterfowl of all kinds including roseate spoonbills and the rare jabiru stork. Estuaries and lagoons where small rivers reach the sea may have a dozen species visible at a time, very near the beach hotel you're staying in. Palo Verde National Park at the mouth of the Tempisque River is a great waterfowl haven that attracts naturalists from many nations.

A biologist from Cornell was studying hummingbirds at Monteverde. Knowing there were several pages of them in my bird book, I asked how many there were in her area. "Thirty species, but only eight common."

When you're watching birds or monkeys in the bush, it's very easy to forget the ground at your feet. Don't. In Rincon de la Vieja National Park I saw my first Rey del Zopilote (king buzzard) in the wild. It's a huge, creamy-white bird with black on the wings and an orange head. I stepped off the horse I'd been riding, camera in hand, and got 4 photos before ants from the hill I was standing on reached and stung my neck! With that lack of care, I was lucky it wasn't a snake.

Guided tours are the easiest way to be sure of seeing certain birds, and may be the only practical way to get to Corcovado National Park, usually reached by charter flight. Audubon, Questers, and others organize these from the United States, often outfitted and led in Costa Rica by **Costa Rica Expeditions**. If you write CRE (address in Appendix), they will tell you who's sending groups.

For these trips or for looking on your own, you'll want binoculars, insect repellent, a shade hat, sunscreen, and good walking shoes. Books printed outside Costa Rica are very expensive with-

14

in the country, so it's worth bringing them with you. Roger Tory Peterson's *Birds of Mexico* is very useful and would be more so if he had illustrated all the birds instead of simply referring to ones shown in his books on Eastern, Western, and Texas birds. For at least the southern half of the country, *Birds of Panama*, by Robert Ridgley, is recommended. The pictures in both of these books are enough to bring any avid birder to Costa Rica.

Howler monkey family takes its noonday break.

Mammals and reptiles in Costa Rica are as diverse as the birds, but generally fewer and much harder to spot. Many are endangered, due more to loss of habitat than overhunting, except in the case of sea turtles. Jaguars, ocelots, marguays, howler, squirrel, spider and capuchin monkeys, sloths, deer, tapirs, peccaries, agoutis, coatimundis, foxes, coyotes, armadillos, and manatees are among the animals. You can see most of them in the zoo in San Jose. Iguanas and alligators are common in some areas. Green turtles nest on the Caribbean coast, primarily at Tortuguero, and leatherback and Pacific Ridley turtles nest on several Pacific beaches.

15

While many of these animals are not only shy but nocturnal, an early morning or early evening watch at a water hole, especially in drier Guanacaste, is a good way to see them. I've seen howler monkeys, storks, and deer in streams beside highway bridges (when someone else was driving). Even in national parks where they do exist, many are rarely seen. Good luck.

The multi-story cloud forest of Monteverde, home of the quetzal and hundreds of other species.

Flora

Costa Rica's flowers, flowering trees and shrubs, and an incredible variety of other tropical plants are a delight to anyone. February and March are the height of the blooming season for trees, including the red Poro tree used for living fence posts along roads.

16

Bromeliads and other plants cover a fallen log on Poás Volcano.

The national flower is an orchid, and there are nearly 1,200 known species of orchids, with some estimates as high as 2,000, in the country. At all seasons, some varieties are in bloom. Finding one beside a trail in the Monteverde forest was a thrill I won't forget. Collecting orchids is done only by government permit, and then you probably couldn't get them back into your home country. Bring a close-up lens and collect them on film!

The annual orchid show in San Jose in March has a fantastic variety. Any time of year you can visit the Lankester orchid gardens, now run by the University of Costa Rica, on the road between Cartgago and Paraiso, open 8 a.m. to 3 p.m.

Within the national parks and in other areas that haven't been deforested, you can enjoy magnificent tropical hardwood trees with huge trunks and spreading branches, often supporting colonies of bromeliads and other plants on branches and trunks. Even in yards everywhere you may find 6-foot samples of shrubs you struggle to grow in tiny pots at home. From landscaped hotel grounds and urban parks to primeval forests and coconut walks along the Caribbean, the variety and colors are thrilling, with surprises on every walk.

17

Narrow gauge train to Puerto Limón crosses steep hillside between coffee plantations. (ICT)

The Train to Puerto Limón

Known as the Northern or Atlantic Railway, this 100-mile narrow-gauge train, completed in 1890, was the key to development of Costa Rica. Until it was built, the country's only export, coffee, had to be hauled by oxcart and pack mule down mountain trails to Puntarenas on the west coast and around Cape Horn by ship to market.

Today the ride from San Jose to Puerto Limón (or the reverse, which takes an additional 2 hours because of the climb) is an unforgettable tour of Costa Rican life and country. You can join a tour run by Swiss Travel which includes a guide, semi-private

18

car, lunch and refreshments, leaving the train at Siquierres to return via a visit to a banana plantation to San Jose in one day. Or you can simply buy a ticket to Limón at the train station at Avenida 3, Calle 21, and climb aboard about 8 a.m. Get the current schedule from ICT or the station. Schedules change, but when I rode, the choice was between the noon "express" run that only made 7 stops and the morning 52-stop "local," both of which arrived at about the same time. I chose the morning, noting that the train would stay still 52 times while I took pictures. Your ticket is a long strip with all the stops printed on it! Try to get a seat on the right side as that's where the best views are until late afternoon just before Limón. If you're traveling on your own, you'll want to bring some food for the 7-hour ride, along with lots of film. Recently, 3 cars, a locomotive and a dining car have been renovated in 1930s style. This special group is scheduled 3 days a week in 1984. There may be an additional charge, but the comfort is worth it.

Some people try to catch the afternoon flight back to San Jose, but the train is often too late for that. If you don't want to stay overnight, you can ride a bus back in 3½ hours, a long day after 6 hours on the train.

This isn't a ride simply to get to the coast. Since the highway was built, the fastest, cheapest way is by bus, but if you go on your own, the train is an awful lot of entertainment for about $2!

The train starts with a whistle and jolts, rattling along through the eastern suburbs of San Jose, between banks covered with blooming red impatiens. You look over plastered walls into backyards as children peer back. After several stops, the train climbs the grade past the national oil storage tanks and drops down into Cartago for a longer stop. More people get on and you continue between the slopes of coffee. At villages of only half a dozen houses clinging to the hill, the train stops and children in freshly washed clothes get on to ride down to the town with the nearest school. They ride the afternoon train home. Vendors board selling food and bottled soda. These villages are here only because of the train, and no road goes near many of them. The barest shacks of rusty sheet metal and scrap lumber have pots of flowering plants hanging or lined up on the porch.

When you think of modern office workers commuting on freeways and living in condominiums traveling this far on vacation for a few days compared with these people living in clean air among their ever-blooming plants on the mountainside overlooking a river roaring in the canyon below, you may wonder who's poor.

The 6-car train pulled by a diesel locomotive rattles and sways around turns so tight you often look out and see the rest of the train. The route looks like a mule trail cut across the steep mountain. Now it crosses a gully and you look almost straight down hundreds of feet into the jungle. Across the Reventazón River tall trees of many species, draped with vines Tarzan might use, extend from river to mountain tops. You wonder how many jaguars and monkeys are watching you!

After several hours you read the fading paint of a station sign and look for its name on your ticket. It's only about 2 inches down the long strip! You stand up and stretch while the train sways on.

Looking down a ravine where the rocks supporting the railroad ties are slung in wire nets over space, you aren't surprised

Coffee ready to pick.

that 6,000 people died building the railway, though malaria in the eastern lowlands was the main killer. The young American, Minor Keith, struggled with the project for nearly 20 years before it was done. When some miles of track were laid from the east coast and money was running short, Keith imported banana seedlings and started the plantations that led to United Fruit Company. Jamaican workers were brought in, as they were more resistant than others to malaria, and were given land along the track.

As the train drops down eastern slopes, you see more and more of their descendants, a large part of the lowland population. These people speak English, making this coast an easy place to travel for those with limited Spanish.

Coffee has now been replaced by sugar cane and bananas, with some groves of cacao, the source of chocolate. At Siquirres, the first major town on the coastal plain, an electric engine replaces the diesel one and you notice the railroad ties are concrete instead of wood. As the train leaves the mountains, you follow the shores of the rushing, muddy Reventazón, occasionally crossing it or clear tributaries on bridges.

Some villages are built up on poles to keep from flooding. In one of the last villages, boardwalks run between houses and the only dry ground seems to be occupied by the cemetery. You pass the national oil refinery at Moin and railroad tracks joining from banana plantations to the north. For a few miles you follow the shore between palms and see breakers in the Caribbean on your left.

Finally the train pulls into Limón and you follow the crowd a few short blocks to the center of town where most hotels and the bus stops are.

The Pacific Railway is an electric train that makes a more modern but very scenic ride from San Jose to Puntarenas on the west coast. It leaves from a station in the southwest corner of San Jose several times a day and takes about 3 hours, twice the time of the bus, but more scenic as it follows river canyons. The station is on Ave. 20 at Calle 2.

Small farm on canal bank, with thatched pole buildings.

"Los Canales"—Inland Waterway

From Moin, a few miles north of Puerto Limón, a jungle waterway extends over 65 miles up the northeast coast to Barra Colorado. Eight rivers form lagoons behind jungle-covered sandbars as they reach the ocean. By digging canals to connect them, the Costa Ricans have built a continuous water highway where there are no land roads. Fishing boats, skiffs, dugout canoes, coconut barges, a government boat and tour boats ply the scenic highway. Traffic varies seasonally according to water depth (less in February and March), fishing and crop seasons.

The ride is spectacular! You glide along a passage sometimes less than 100 feet wide between banks lined with palms and jungle. Water hyacinths cover water near the shores. Turtles sun themselves on logs and an occasional alligator splashes into the water just as you get your camera focussed. You pass a family of howler monkeys in a treetop and later a trio of brown spider monkeys swinging effortlessly from one limb to another. A dozen white egrets take off from a tree ahead. A huge blue-green

kingfisher swoops beside the boat. The boat driver points at a
treetop and you peer but don't see anything move. Nothing does
—it's a sloth hanging spread-eagled by the front and back feet
on the same side. At least there's no rush to get the picture. The
tree's leaves move in the breeze, but the sloth doesn't.

Three-toed sloth hangs for hours in tree above canal.

Occasionally you pass a small farm or a thatched hut with a
pig standing on the canal bank and a housewife washing clothes
in the water. Standard yellow highway signs note the kilometers
to villages at river intersections. At Parismina, Tortuguero, and
Barra Colorado, there are fishing lodges where tarpon and
snook fishermen fly in from San Jose for a few days to a week.
Tortuguero is a village described in the Eastern region later in
this book. If you're not on a tour going farther, you may want to
stop over here. Just north of the village is the river mouth where
waves break in the Caribbean. You turn left up another river
channel and pass a hill on the right, the only one for miles. This
is Tortuguero National Park, refuge for the green turtle, the
manatee, and many other species. For more details, see the section on that park.

Soon you leave the river and follow a palm-lined canal
straight for miles with poetic reflections in the dark bog water.
Against the afternoon sky a silhouette crosses ahead—it looks
like a bird attached to a canoe—a toucan! The first time you see
one outside a cage is a real thrill. Great blue herons and small
night herons wade near shore until you approach before
flying off.

This ride ends at the village of Barra Colorado, the mouth of the Rio Colorado. One can hope that Nicaragua's political and military situation will calm down soon so you can continue on a tour boat or perhaps a local boat (though there is lots less traffic in that direction at any time) up the Rio San Juan, which forms the Costa Rican border, up the beautiful clear Serapiqui to the village of Puerto Viejo and thence by rough road back to San Jose.

Highway signs for a water highway direct boats at river intersections.

Presently your choices for the ride I've described are by tour boat, government launch ("La Samay"), or by making your own arrangements with freight boats. My first trip up this waterway was in a fast, narrow, and very unstable fish-hauling boat that makes the round trip from Barra to Moin and back in a day. Night came very black with rain showers as the driver peered through a slit in the plastic before him and steered around logs I couldn't see, occasionally switching on a dim flashlight to shine at boats we met. No navigation lights on shore here—any flashing light was a firefly! Cheapest and slowest are the "coco-boats" which haul coconuts to Moin and people with their shopping back. Built like powered barges, they make the African Queen look quite seaworthy. The government boat runs several days a week (starting very early in the morning from Moin) when water depth permits. It has a schedule which you may be able to get from the ICT office under the Cultural Plaza in San Jose. If you're using any of the other local boats, you need to have flexible enough time to allow an extra day or two in case there aren't any boats leaving north or south the day you want to go. You can also check with SANSA, the internal airline, to see if they have flights to Barra Colorado or Tortuguero on the days you want to go. They do, however, cancel if they don't have enough passengers. Charter flights can be arranged from the airport in San Jose and the fishing lodges at Tortuguero and Barra Colorado use them.

Tour boats are the most predictable way to go if your trip is scheduled. They also stop for wildlife photos. The guides are looking for animals and know where they are most likely **Rio Colorado Lodge** at Barra Colorado runs several trips weekly from San Jose on their modern tour boat, with a short stop at Tortuguero, using a mini-bus between San Jose and Moin and charter flights between Barra and San Jose. You may do this loop in either direction, depending on their schedule. The tour takes 2 days, but you can stay extra days at the lodge or ride the train to Limón, stay overnight, and join a tour there if you've booked it before leaving San Jose.

Alligator suns on a log before diving under as we approach.

25

Avid wildlife watchers with more time will possibly see a greater variety of species by going on a nature tour run several times a year by **Costa Rica Expeditions** paddling back channels with quiet boats led by biologists. These are usually in the Tortuguero area. Note that **Rio Colorado** is the only one of the fishing lodges which stays open all year. The others are open for snook in the fall and tarpon in winter and early spring.

A hooked sailfish leaps from the water on Costa Rica's west coast. (ICT)

Fishing

Costa Rica has some of the world's finest sport fishing on both coasts and in streams and lakes. Depending on season and location, you can choose among tarpon, snook, marlin, sailfish, yellowfin tuna, roosterfish, wahoo, crevalle, snapper, or often hook several species in a day. In fresh water, rainbow trout have been planted, and bobo and guapote are native. The fishing lodges and sportfishing clubs hold tournaments (ICT has the dates).

26

Facilities are increasing for fishermen, with new lodges, more charter boats, and a large corps of knowledgeable guides on both coasts. For scuba fishermen, equipment and air refills are now available at major resorts on the west coast as well as in San Jose. You will need a fishing license which your lodge can get for you (they need your name, marital status, address, and passport number) or which you can get from the Dept. of Agriculture (Ministerio de Agricultura y Ganaderia, C. 1, Av. 1, San Jose, Costa Rica. Phone 23-08-29).

You should bring a wide-brimmed hat, long-sleeved shirts, long pants, and a *good* sunscreen. On the Caribbean coast, bring light rain wear all year. You are encouraged to bring your own gear, but lodges can arrange rentals. Generally for saltwater fishing, you need 20 lb. test line or stronger. ICT has a brochure on fishing that lists recommended lures. Your lodge can be more specific. The fishing columnist for the *Tico Times* sometimes publishes recommendations.

The Caribbean coast is best known for tarpon and snook, with much of the fishing done from skiffs in river channels. Tarpon average 75 lbs., though larger ones are common. Fishermen rave about hooking more than a dozen a day even in November which is considered off-season. The main tarpon season is January through mid-May, though they are caught all year. However, even Archie Fields, owner of **Rio Colorado Lodge**, does not recommend the rains of December as enjoyable fishing weather.

Snook, a fine gamefish and good food, is caught on both coasts, near river mouths and from beaches. Peak season for large ones is from August to mid-October, but they are caught all year.

Most fishing lodges are open only for the seasons listed above (see their descriptions in the Eastern region later in this book), except for the **Rio Colorado Lodge**. At Tortuguero, **Sabina's Cabinas** and other rooms are open all year, and you could make your own fishing arrangements with a guide and skiff. The **Tortuga Lodge** is open for main fishing seasons.

On the Pacific coast, sailfish and marlin are the most sought fish. Tamarindo and Coco Beaches both have boats and guides

A fisherman stands beside the tarpon he caught near Rio Colorado Lodge.

available, and most hotels anywhere along the coast can arrange deep-sea fishing. Sailfish average 100 lbs. but are often larger. Marlin can be huge, and are found from Golfito north. Peak seasons listed in Jerry Ruhlow's column in the *Tico Times*, July 13, 1984, are as follows: Sailfish—July through September; marlin—January, February, May, July, August and September; roosterfish—year round but most caught in May and June; dorado (dolphinfish)—same as sailfish; wahoo—June through September; yellowfin tuna—July and August, but caught all year.

Freshwater fish seasons vary. Lake Arenal is especially popular for guapote (there is at least 1 tournament a year) and the season is open January 1 through September 30.

The avid fisherman can find fish all year in Costa Rica and can find peak season for at least 1 species almost any time.

Travel agents in the United States and elsewhere book package tours to the fishing lodges and you will find the addresses of the lodges themselves in the Eastern, Northwestern, and Western sections later in this book.

Hunting

The days of unlimited sport hunting for jaguars and other exotic species are over in Costa Rica and most other places. As tropical forests everywhere are converted to crop or rangeland, the remaining habitat will not allow a surplus for hunting. Most species formerly hunted in Latin America are now threatened or endangered.

In Costa Rica there is legal hunting by permit for doves and ducks on their winter range—some of the same birds you see on spring and fall migrations in North America. The dryland rice fields of Guanacaste are the hunting area, from November through March. Hunters sometimes get 140 doves in a day, usually given to the nearby villagers for food. Hunters stay in or near Nicoya. For package tours or information, write Archie Fields, owner of the **Rio Colorado Lodge**, who holds permits for the area. His address and phone are listed in the information sources section.

Costa Ricans love soccer games and play in every village. This is a Sunday afternoon match between Santa Ana and a Heredia team.

Sports

Costa Ricans are avid sportsmen and have built many facilities throughout the country. Some are basic. A few are lavish. There

29

are local and international tournaments in several sports, so you can be a spectator or participant according to your interests. *Soccer* (futbol)—almost every village with a bit of flat ground has a soccer field, often in front of the church. After work and on weekends, there's almost always play. Major games and tournaments are played at Sabana Park at the west end of San Jose. Newspaper sport sections always carry the latest soccer results.

Basketball—is also popular, with major games played at the national gymnasium in Sabana Park. There are baskets for practice in the park and in most villages.

Swimming—Besides the beaches and rivers, most major hotels and apartotels have pools. Sabana Park has an Olympic-size pool, as does the Cariari Country Club. The pools fed by Oja de Agua spring south of Juan Santamaria Airport, are colder but unchlorinated due to the large supply of fresh water. There are major swim meets and a well-organized junior racing program at Sabana Park and Cariari Country Club.

Golf—Cariari Country Club, a few miles west of San Jose, has the only 18-hole golf course in Costa Rica. Designed by a major golf course architect, it's the site of international tournaments featuring many PGA pros. There are also 4 9-hole courses: at the Costa Rican Country Club in Escazú; surrounding the Golfito Airport; at Los Reyes Country Club near Alajuela; and at El Castillo Country Club above Heredia. Most have equipment available, but at the older, less formal Golfito course built as a recreation facility for banana workers, one of the hotel owners said she could arrange for use of the only bag of clubs in town.

Tennis—Several of the deluxe hotels have courts as do Sabana Park, the nearby Costa Rica Tennis Club, the Cariari Country Club (where the World Friendship Tournament is played in March and April), the Costa Rica Country Club, and the Los Reyes Country Club. The Costa Rica Tennis Club and Sabana Park courts are close to San Jose.

Horseback riding—Costa Rica raises very fine jumpers and parade horses, notably Andalusian and Paso Fino horses with the soft gait prized by the Spaniards. On early mornings in the suburbs of Santa Ana and Escazú you may see them in the streets.

30

Magnificent bay horse at Hipíco La Caraña west of San Jose. Jumping and polo are featured here.

During Christmas week, there is the Horse Parade in downtown San Jose with over 1000 of the country's finest. Near San Jose you can take instruction and ride at Hípico La Caraña, about 15 miles west of the city, and at the Cariari Country Club. At Cariari, jumping, equitation, and dressage are featured with expert instruction and 4 to 7 day clinics. Horseshows are frequent. Elsewhere you can rent country horses, and many hotels will arrange it for you. Note that on the coasts where it is often hot, riding early or late may be more fun than at midday.

Rodeos and Bullfights—Guanacaste is the cattle country of Costa Rica, with the festivals and sports that go with it. Rodeos and bullfights are frequent during the dry season from November to April, in Santa Cruz, Nicoya, and Liberia. In Costa Rican bullfights, the bull is not killed, and the whole show is for fun! During Christmas holidays there are rodeos and bullfights in San Jose. Rodeos are also held at the Cariari Country Club.

Bicycling—Bicycle touring and racing is a major sport in Costa Rica. The big event of the year is the "Vuelta a Costa Rica" in December, lasting 12 days and crisscrossing the mountain back-

31

bone of the country several times, from sea level to over 11,000 feet. It attracts cyclists from many countries, including the United States. The Recreational Cycling Association plans family outings which many join on Sundays.

A friend who has cycled long distances here says that drivers are more considerate of cyclists than he expected and give room when passing. He warns that one needs to be prepared for heat and great temperature changes with altitude. He carries liquids and a gas mask for long grades also used by diesel trucks and buses. Despite heat and fumes at times, he recommends cycling in Costa Rica.

Other Sports—Wrestling, in the national gymnasium at Sabana Park, car and motorcycle racing at La Guácima near Alajuela, volleyball everywhere, baseball and Little League programs, and jogging for everyone on the paths at Sabana Park are a few of the other sports you can watch and participate in.

Theater and Museums

These are almost all in San Jose or its suburbs, though historical and archeological sites are scattered throughout the country.

The National Theater is Costa Rica's symbol of the people's interest in the arts as well as the national architectural treasure. A European opera company, led by singer Adelina Patti, came to Guatemala City in the late 1800's but didn't travel on to Costa Rica because there was no suitable place to perform. In response, the coffee growers agreed to pay a tax on coffee they exported to raise money for a theater. Construction started in 1890 and the building was finished in 1897.

Today it is one of the busiest buildings in the country, with performances or official functions 320 days a year. If your Spanish is good, enjoy one of the many plays presented by Costa Rican and touring foreign companies. With little or no Spanish, you can watch dance performances, opera, or the National Symphony. Check the schedule of upcoming events so you won't miss the ones you'd like during your stay. Tickets are amazingly inexpensive, many under $2.

The National Museum in San Jose was formerly the Army barracks and still has bullet scars from the 1948 revolution. Costa Rica is proud of having turned the military facility to such a peaceful, cultural use.

The theater is patterned after European opera houses though on a smaller, more comfortable scale. The facade, overlooking a rose garden and a tree-shaded square, is Renaissance style, with figures representing Music, Fame, and Dance. Statues of Beethoven and Calderon de la Barca fill niches on either side of the entrance. The lobby inside has marble floors and columns. To your left is a refreshment area with coffee and great ice cream concoctions, its walls usually adorned with art exhibits. The grand staircase and foyer on the second floor feature Italian marble sculptures, paintings and a mural of Costa Rica's main exports. You can tour the building with or without a guide during the day, but shouldn't miss the experience of a performance. Av. 2, C.3., adjacent to the Cultural Plaza and **Gran Hotel Costa Rica.**

The National Theater adjoins the south side of the Cultural Plaza and faces the same square as the Gran Hotel Costa Rica.

Other smaller theaters are around the San Jose area and the University of Costa Rica campus. Check the English language *Tico Times*, weekly on Fridays, for performances, locations and for art exhibits in the city which change often.

The National Museum of Costa Rica is in the old army barracks on Calle 17, Avenida 2/ctl (see the San Jose section for an explanation of San Jose street addresses). Phones, 22-12-29 and 21-02-95. Open Tuesday through Saturday, 8:30 to 5:00. Closed Mondays. Sundays and holidays, 9:00 to 5:00. Small admission fee. Students with identification free. The outside walls of this fortress still show bullet scars from the revolution of 1948, after which the army was abolished. The museum features an excellent exhibit of pre-Columbian artifacts, historical exhibits from the colonial period, and historical religious costumes and articles. All of Costa Rica's history and historical art are represented here in the massive stone buildings surrounding a garden.

The Jade Museum features prehistoric carvings of jade and stone, and some ceramic and gold articles, arranged according to their region and historical period. It's on the 11th floor of the INS (Institute for National Security) Building, Calle 9, Av. 7.

The National Theater, Costa Rica's architectural treasure and one of its busiest buildings, with performances some 320 days a year.

Phone, 23-58-00. Open Tuesday through Sunday, 8:00 to 5:00. Admission free. Despite the hours listed above, I was told it was too late when I tried to enter once at 3 p.m. You should probably call ahead or check with the ICT office under the Cultural Plaza. Note that most museum openings are early in Costa Rica. Closings sometimes are as well.

The Gold Museum has recently moved from the Banco Central de Costa Rica to a much more accessible location near the ICT information center under the Cultural Plaza on Av. Central. Hours not known. This collection, one of the finest in the world, contains over 1600 pieces of all sizes and types. The artistic wealth as well as the gold make it well worth a visit. Many of the articles were obtained from private collections of burial and religious art.

The National Art Museum occupies the former airport terminal building in Sabana Park on Calle 42 at the west end of Paseo Colon. Phones, 23-60-87 and 22-86-04. Open Tuesdays through Sundays, 10:00 to 5:00. Closed Mondays. In this lovely Spanish-style building is a great collection of some of the most expressive art you'll ever see. Most is modern, but some sculptures are pre-Columbian. There are changing exhibits as well as the permanent collection.

The Natural Science Museum is in the Colegio La Salle, a school at the southwest of Sabana Park. Phone 32-64-27. Open Mondays through Fridays, 8:00 to 3:00. Small admission charge. All specimens and scenes were prepared locally, though they feature species from around the world as well as Costa Rica.

The Entomology Museum in Sabanilla Montes de Oca, an eastern suburb of San Jose, is the only insect museum in Central America. The butterflies alone would be worth a trip. Phone 25-55-55. Hours not known. Call the museum or ask the ICT.

The Orosí Valley. (ICT)

COSTA RICA—THE NATION

Geography and Climate

With a land area of about 19,700 square miles, Costa Rica is the second smallest country in Central America, after El Salvador. Its rapidly growing population of about 2½ million is the second smallest as well, after Panama. It forms a land bridge with coasts on both the Atlantic and Pacific oceans between Nicaragua and Panama.

The Atlantic Coast is a lowland, rather straight and with few good harbors, about 125 miles long. The Pacific Coast has 2 deep bays formed by the Nicoya and Osa Peninsulas, and is over 600 miles long. The ports of Puntarenas, with the new port at Caldera just to the south, and Golfito in the southwest corner of the country are in these bays. Many of the beaches we've mentioned line this coast.

36

Costa Rica has a mountainous backbone running the length of the country with just one very significant break, the Meseta Central or Central Valley. The northern mountains are a chain of volcanoes extending south from Nicaragua, including the Cordilleras Guanacaste, Tilaran and Central. Within this chain are active and dormant volcanoes, thermal springs, and many cinder cones. It's a very active zone with eruptions, earthquakes, and some moving lava flows. South of the Meseta Central is the Talamanca Range topped by Cerra Chirripó over 12,600 ft. high, continuing south into Panama.

The Meseta Central is by far the most important area of the country though it's only about 15 by 40 miles. This rolling area of rich volcanic soils has a spring climate all year thanks to its altitude of about 4,000 feet. Frost never happens and the main seasonal variation is rain. Temperatures vary widely according to altitude, with a few hundred feet making a real difference. Here two-thirds of the people live and it's one of the most heavily populated areas in Latin America.

Some people have described Costa Rica as "the Meseta Central and everywhere else." The bustling capital of San Jose, with 275,000 people in 1983, and the nearby towns of Heredia, Alajuela, Cartago and Turrialba, plus a swarm of smaller villages, are indeed the center of government, industry, agriculture, and most important, outlook, of Costa Rica.

South of the Meseta Central, bordering the western flank of the Talamanca Mountains, is the Valle de General, with its principal town of San Isidro de General. While it is much lower and warmer than the Meseta Central, it isn't as crowded, and many farmers have moved into the area recently since the Inter-American Highway and the new road down the west coast from Esparza have connected this area more closely to domestic and international trade. No roads cross the Talamancas and few lead far into them.

The Nicoya and Osa Peninsulas have central ranges of hills to 3000 ft., with some of the Nicoya hills being quite steep. The western coastal plain is generally rolling rather than truly flat, and extends from the Panamanian border northward, widening to form the cattle and rice country of Guanacaste, to the Nicaraguan border. Similarly, the eastern plain widens from south to north, forming a wide northern and eastern lowland north of Puerto Limón. The lowlands have a limited population, mostly in agriculture, few large towns, but do have some larger fincas or plantations.

Costa Rica extends from 8° to 11° north of the Equator, so the sun is never far from overhead (it actually passes over during May and September). The length of daylight hours varies only slightly all year and the average daily temperature in a given location may vary only a few degrees throughout the year. In San Jose, the daily highs are in the 70's, Fahrenheit, almost all year. Alajuela, just a few hundred feet lower, averages a few degrees warmer, while Limón and Puntarenas at sea level are usually in the high 80's or 90's during "summer," December through March. There is much greater variation, especially in the mountains, between day and night temperatures at the same place. You will usually want a sweater or jacket at night in San Jose, and I wore one on a rainy night in a leaky boat in the Tortuguero Canals, at sea level.

Tug pushes ferry barge with cattle trucks across the Gulf of Tempisque.

38

Altitude rather than season really controls temperature here. Frosts do occur on Chirripó, and most of the country above 6500 ft. is in cloud forest, cool with fog or rain brought by the northeast trade winds. Mornings are often clear in the mountains, with clouds building in early afternoon.

Those of you who've joined the metric world will find the distances, altitudes and temperatures as given in Costa Rica easy. This U.S. resident has not yet learned to think metric, and so in this first edition will use miles, feet, and Fahrenheit, with apologies for any confusion.

Rainy and dry seasons and the amount of rainfall are controlled by the northeast trades, and the doldrums (a tropical zone of rising air which follows the sun north and south), and the mountain chain running through Costa Rica. The dry season in San Jose and the West is usually December into April (May in Guanacaste) while it runs from January to April on the Atlantic Coast. While the east coast is wetter, some areas on the west get extra rain because of being aligned with passes which allow the moist winds through. A station in the eastern mountains reported rain on 359 days in one year! However on the drier northwest coast, there are few rainy days even in the wet season, and the rain then is generally in late afternoon or night.

Even rainy season shouldn't stop you if you allow for it. On October mornings in San Jose I enjoyed the clear moist air, Poás Volcano with its steam plume against the blue sky, and flocks of chattering parrots passing overhead. All morning and much of the afternoon stayed dry, though clouds gathered. By late afternoon almost every day, the sky burst. Everyone still out unfolded the umbrellas they always carry. I liked sitting on the roofed porch watching the rain gauge fill and overflow.

Golfito in the southwest actually has a climate much like the Caribbean coast, due to the mountains vs. the winds. One December evening there even an umbrella didn't help much in the 4 inches of rain that fell in 2 hours, but it was warm and the rain cooled the town after a hot sunny day.

Costa Rican Holidays

January 1, New Year's Day
March 19, St. Joseph
Easter, 3 days (at least)
April 11, Battle of Rivas
May 1, Labor Day
June, Corpus Christi
June 29, St. Peter and St. Paul
July 25, Guanacaste Day
August 2, Virgin of Los Angeles
August 15, Mothers' Day
September 15, Independence Day
October 12, Columbus Day
December 8, Conception of the Virgin
December 25, Christmas Day
December 28-31, San Jose only.

While these are the official days, during Christmas holiday week between Christmas and New Year's, and during Easter Holy Week, most of the country seems to be shut down. Those who can take vacation then, and the more accessible beaches are jammed. Columbus Day is the time of the annual festival in Limón, and the August 2 holiday of the Virgin of Los Angeles is Cartago's biggest festival. Some celebrants march from San Jose to Cartago!

The road up Irazú, with its hairpin turns, has many fine views over Cartago and the Meseta Central.

SEASONS & ACTIVITIES	D	J	F	M	A	M	J	J	A	S	O	N
Rainy season, San Jose					–	–	x	x	x	x	x	x
Dry season, San Jose	x	x	x	x	x	–						
Rainy season, Guanacaste					–	–	x	x	x	x	x	x
Dry season, Guanacaste	x	x	x	x	x	–						
Rainy season, Limón	x	x			x	x		x			x	x
Dry season, Limón			x	x				x		x	x	
Independence Day										15		
Carnivals	S.J.					Punt.					Limón	
Horse Shows	S.J.											
Rodeos, Guanacaste		18	x						25			
Bullfights		18	x						25			
Tarpon, East Coast		x	x	x	x	x	x	x	x	x	x	x
Snook, East Coast		x	x	x	x	x	x	x	x	x	x	x
Marlin, West Coast	x	x	x	x	x	x	x	x	x	x	x	x
Sailfish, West Coast	←------- NORTH -------→					←------- SOUTH -------→						
Tortuguero												
Green Turtles, egglaying								x	x	x		
Green Turtles, hatching									x	x	x	
Guanacaste												
Leatherback, egg laying								x	x	x	x	
Leatherback, hatching									x	x	x	x
Ridley egg laying										x	x	
Dove hunting, Guanacaste	x	x	x	x								x
Duck hunting, Guanacaste	x	x	x	x								x

Spanish-style fort tower built 100 years ago, in Heredia.

Prehistoric basaltic balls including this one have been found near Palmar Nord. No one knows who carved them or why, but some very large ones are nearly true spheres.

Pre-Columbian stone figure. (ICT)

History

This section will give only the briefest outline of Costa Rican history, to give some perspective to what you will see. For more information and an excellent discussion of social and political conditions, you could read *The Costa Ricans* by Richard, Karen and Mavis Biesanz, who have lived in Costa Rica for years.

43

Before the Spaniards came, Costa Rica had several dozen independent tribes who apparently didn't form the empires that the Mayas, Aztecs, and Incas did to the north and south of them. They did some farming and did have some permanent settlements which are still being studied. The sculptures and ceramic figures you can see in museums show that they had artists and had developed culture.

In 1502 Columbus landed at Cariari, now Puerto Limón, and stayed for several days. The Indians showed his men some gold, and he felt there was hope for more.

However the small tribes hadn't accumulated the wealth that drew the Spaniards to the bigger empires. Warfare between the tribes and with the Spaniards plus the diseases brought by the white men to which the natives had no immunity nearly wiped out the native population.

The Spanish who came and settled found both coasts had a hot, humid climate and tropical diseases which many couldn't tolerate. The coasts were also raided by pirates of many countries, especially British, who sacked and burned whatever the settlers had. There were no easy routes to the interior, but eventually small farmers did settle up in the cool, healthful climate of the Meseta Central.

Unlike the other Spanish colonies, these settlers had no way to amass great wealth, no natives to enslave, and few to intermarry. These farmers remained almost pure Spanish and didn't develop the social classes or the mestizo majority that characterized most of New Spain. They were almost forgotten by Spain since they had little to trade and no wealth to send back to Europe. Even the access routes to their settlements mostly led up from the west coast instead of the east.

Cartago was the main town, started in 1563, but San Jose wasn't established until 1737, Heredia in 1717. The population, mostly poor and still struggling, hadn't grown enough to settle the whole valley, though they had brought some fine cattle and horses from Spain and continued to grow livestock and food crops.

In the late 1700s coffee was introduced, and with the rich volcanic soils and near perfect climate, it was a winner! Land was given to those who would plant it for an export crop. Even though the coffee had to be carried by oxcart west to Puntarenas and thence around Cape Horn or across Panama, Costa Rica finally began to grow in population and wealth.

In 1821 the Spanish colonies declared independence from Spain. Various attempts were made to unify the former colonies in the Central American Federation which Costa Rica joined in 1824 and from which she withdrew in 1838. The lack of rapid communication as well as differing interests made a unified regional government very difficult, though economic and political treaties based on regional interests have been signed.

Coffee growth and trade led some families to become richer and more powerful than others, and Costa Rica was no longer a classless society. It was still a group of small towns and farms with little feeling of nationality. The town councils met separately and rivalries grew until San Jose won a battle with Cartago and the capital was moved to San Jose in 1823.

The casona at Santa Rosa National Park. Here Costa Rican volunteers surrounded William Walker and his filibusters and drove them out of Costa Rica.

Democracy developed with some setbacks according to the personalities of those who were elected chief of state, and then president after 1847. Some of the most autocratic leaders are remembered for starting schools and getting roads and railroads built. Juan Rafael Mora, president 1849-59, recruited an army of volunteers which marched from San Jose to Santa Rosa (now a national park) to surround and drive out pro-slavery American William Walker and his band of filibusters who were trying to establish a slavery empire in Central America. Walker and his band were driven back into Nicaragua and again defeated at the Battle of Rivas. National hero, Juan Santamaria, was a youth from Alajuela who volunteered to torch the building Walker and his men occupied, knowing it was a suicide mission. Walker was later captured in Honduras, held by the British, and turned over to Honduran authorities who executed him. President Mora's proclamation of the rights of the Costa Rican people to be free of foreign despots is respected by Costa Ricans as U.S. citizens respect the Declaration of Independence.

In 1889 for the first time Costa Rica's election was not controlled by the party in power (nearly a hundred years later many other nations still haven't reached this point). Later administrations have passed laws establishing national health insurance, labor rights, and property rights.

The last internal military strife was in 1948 when the party in power tried to use the army to remain so after losing an election. A volunteer group led by Jose Figueres took Cartago, and after widespread violence and bloodshed, a cease-fire was arranged. Costa Ricans were determined this should never happen again. Among the changes Figueres and his followers enacted were limitations on the length of presidential terms and elimination of the army. A well-armed and trained national guard serves as the country's police force. Its control is turned over to the election tribunal before national elections to remove it from politics and guarantee free elections.

In recent years the population, size of bureaucracy, and foreign debt have grown rapidly. With almost all exports in the form of raw agricultural products, Costa Rica is at the mercy of the world prices for them and for the oil it needs. The International Monetary Fund places stringent conditions on economic policy in an effort to control the foreign debt. The traveler who checks the prices in stores will quickly discover the difference between products from Central America and those imported.

Meanwhile the political and military turmoil in all the Central American countries to the north has added tension in Costa Rica. These people are keenly aware that they have something in education, personal freedom, and the possibility for personal progress that few in Latin America have. President Luis Alberto Monge has used the increased world attention to the region to make others aware of Costa Rica and what it stands for. Many other countries now provide research funds, economic aid, and increased trade.

Ojo De Agua fills swimming pools with clean, unchlorinated water. It's a favorite weekend treat for Costa Rican families.

Social Conditions

"Tell them Costa Rica is different," many people said, from truck drivers to government department heads. They're right.

47

Where else can you see this from 20,000 feet? Fly over El Salvador and you'll see big fields with a cluster of small houses and one big house. Fly over Costa Rica and you'll see many small fields and villages with houses that look similar from that distance, especially in the Meseta Central. Plantations owned by the banana companies and some of the cattle fincas in Guanacaste are an exception, but not as prevalent as in the other countries.

A walk through San Jose will show you that there are rich and poor here, but most people are middle class. Costa Rica has the largest proportion of middle class in Latin America. That, coupled with its high literacy rate (elementary and secondary education are free and elementary attendance is required) are the foundation of its democracy. Ride a public bus at evening rush hour and you'll see everyone reading newspapers.

Ticos, as the Costa Ricans call themselves, are very clean and very well-dressed. Their families, usually large, are all-important in their lives. For many, the extended family is the source of all their social life. Children are loved extravagantly and with endless patience. You rarely see a crying child. They grow up to be cheerful, considerate people who will do anything to help you—as long as you're polite. They aren't subservient. Cheerful self-respect you'll see everywhere, among the Spanish in the Meseta Central, the Indians and mestizos of Guanacaste, and the blacks of the Caribbean coast.

Costa Rica is not immune to the human problems of the 20th century or of the developing nations. It is a nation of hard-working people who from earliest colonial times have struggled to make as good a life as possible for themselves and their families. Compared with the TV generation in other places, their resourcefulness in having fun on a minimum of money is impressive. With their families at home or on outings, they find fun or make it.

Population growth and the conversion of field agriculture to cattle range and bananas to palm nuts which take less labor have forced many into cities and towns looking for work. Everywhere there is a serious shortage of low-cost housing, though the government has built thousands of units near San Jose. In the outlying areas, and particularly among the people of the Caribbean

48

coast, there is a distrust of what the government and population majority in the Meseta Central may do that affects their life and land. Many women, especially the younger ones, feel caught between the traditional Spanish stereotype of their submissive role and the opportunities that are (or they feel should be) open to them. More women are studying for the professions, especially law. The San Jose area is more liberal than the conservative countryside in the choices open to women. You will find many in offices, occasionally even as "la directora."

As I noted earlier, Costa Rica is dedicated to solving these problems and has done much to make its citizens' lives better. Some solutions may wait until the growth of population and the bureaucracy is slowed.

Agriculture

Early agriculture in the tropics was the slash and burn type, with small areas of forest cut and planted for a few years before the soil was depleted and the farmer cleared another plot. Heavy tropical rains and the rapid breakdown of compost at these temperatures limit fertility unless fertilizers are added or crops rotated, or a volcano periodically adds mineral-rich ash to the upper layer.

Cloud of egrets fly up from pasture with grazing Brahma cattle in Guanacaste.

Coffee and bananas were the first two major exports of Costa Rica. Coffee still makes up 20% of the country's agricultural production though it's concentrated in a small proportion of the land and subject to wild price fluctuations on the world market. Throughout the Meseta Central you'll see the glossy green bushes, often shaded by scattered trees. In season the white blossoms or red berries add to the beauty.

Bananas were first grown on the east coast along the railroad during construction, partly to help pay for completion of the project. That was the start of the United Fruit Company. Later the Panama disease damaged many plantations and new planting was done on the southwest coast. Some western plantations are now being converted to oil palm—the oil is used in margarine. You may want to try varieties of bananas you can find in markets here which have much more flavor than the bombproof ones bred for shipping overseas. They make good snacks to take on buses and trains.

In the past 20 years, beef has become the third largest export, grown mostly in the west. Cattle are Brahma purebred or cross, bred to take heat and insects. (Dairy cattle are raised only in the highlands usually above the Meseta Central or at Monteverde.) Some cattle fincas in Guanacaste use introduced African grasses and modern methods to increase production. Almost all the beef is grass-fed and relatively lean, exported mostly for fast-food hamburger and TV dinners. Costa Rica desperately needs foreign exchange, but she is paying a high price for it. The tropical forests that protected soil on steep hills and watersheds are being cut and burned to provide short-term rangeland until the soil is too eroded or depleted. The government is becoming concerned as are many citizens, and one can hope that improved breeding and pasture methods on appropriate land can replace deforestation on steep hills or remaining virgin forests.

Sugar has long been a major crop for home use and export. You'll see it along the road and train in the eastern Meseta Central. There it grows between coffee fields until it becomes the major crop as you drop down past Turrialba and into banana country. Other export crops are pineapples, copra from dried coconuts, cacao, cotton, and palm oil. A new industry, growing rapidly in the Meseta Central, is cut flowers and house plants,

Banana stem hanging from tree.

flown to Europe and North America. Rice is a major crop in the
west, all of it used in the country as it's a staple in the local diet.
Also grown for local consumption are beans, corn, honey, vege-
tables, mangoes, papayas (and many other tropical fruits), pork,
chickens, and potatoes (mostly on the slopes of Irazú).

Lately there have been several developments promoting new
export crops—oranges for juice concentrate, jojoba for oil, and
macadamia nuts, to name several. If you stay in deluxe San Jose
hotels, you'll be offered information about investments in these.

Surge tower controls water pressure at Arenal hydroelectric plant. Arenal generates power for Costa Rica and exports to Nicaragua and El Salvador.

Industry

Costa Rica is one of the world's largest per capita producers of hydroelectric power with big installations at Lakes Arenal and Cachí. It exports electric power to several other Central American countries. Though there has been some oil exloration and talk of a trans-Costa Rican pipeline to transport Alaskan and Venezuelan oil, presently there is no oil produced in the country, which has made balancing the economy difficult. Costa Rica is offering incentives to labor-intensive industries producing items for export. Several plants import textiles and export finished products such as underwear. One successful operator imports used typewriters from North America, reconditions them in a modern plant and exports them wholesale all over Latin America. There's plenty of room for imagination here! There are many products that Costa Rica would rather produce internally than pay foreign exchange for, but with a well-scattered population only as big as a large city, there isn't the market to make it pay.

The major non-agricultural industry (aside from government) is tourism. While numbers have dropped recently due to political problems to the north, Costa Rica has attractions and enough tourist facilities including hotels, restaurants and tour operators to handle many more. Costa Rica has so much to offer the tourist, and does it so well, that it is rapidly being discovered by thousands who ride jets instead of tossing Spanish galleons.

The former airport terminal and control tower at Sabana Park is now the national art museum, with very moving exhibits.

PLANNING YOUR TRIP

Do you hope to see as much as possible in the time you have for this trip, or would you rather "sit and watch the coconuts fall," as a relaxed friend in sleepy Puerto Viejo put it?

On my first trip to Costa Rica, I had not had a vacation in 8 years and really needed to get away from lists of things I had to do. I chose Costa Rica because it was an interesting place I hadn't been, with lots of birds and wildlife where no one shot at you. If the tropical heat proved too much after years of living in Alaska, I could go up to the cloud forests and look for quetzals. Planning for everything from snorkeling to high altitudes of course made packing harder.

San Jose, nearly in the center of the country, is a well-located base for touring. With 23 days to spend, I flew into San Jose and spent several days there learning my way around and getting bus, train, and boat schedules. Any hotel in San Jose will store extra baggage while you travel if they know you're coming back to stay there. Leaving dressy and warmer clothes there, I traveled a lop-sided figure 8 with a loop on each coast, and returned to San Jose for a few days in the middle and at the end of my trip. From San Jose I rode public buses up Irazú and Poás, toured Cartago and Alajuela, and went to the bird zoo. In San Jose I toured museums and the national zoo and attended performances of the National Symphony and a Venezuelan dance troupe in the National Theater.

I rode the train to Puerto Limón, spent a night there, and rode the bus to the village of Cahuita. It was so peaceful that I spent 4 days, staying in a primitive but clean cabina, snorkeling and birdwatching in the national park. Back by bus to Limón for another night because there wasn't any boat that day. Then up the canales for 2 days at Barra Colorado before riding boat and bus back to San Jose.

The electric train west to Puntarenas didn't go when I wanted to, so I rode the bus and spent 2 nights there. I enjoyed the Calypso tour in the Gulf of Nicoya and caught the early morning ferry the next day to the Nicoya Peninsula. There are more direct routes to Liberia and Santa Rosa National Park, but I wanted to see the country. The bus dropped me at the park entrance and I hiked into the campground and spent 3 days hiking, swimming, and wildlife watching before returning by bus to San Jose.

I've never seen so much or learned so much in 23 days! However, the stops for several days helped keep the trip from being a race. With all that travel and camping out just 2 nights, I spend an average of $17 a day for everything but souvenirs. You can spent a great deal more, or somewhat less if you stay more in one place.

What are your interests? What kind of trip do *you* want?

Exchange

Please note: you need the current exchange rate compared to your own currency to plan and budget your trip. That rate was 42.10 colones per US $1 during most of the research for this book. You can get the current rate from the nearest Costa Rican consulate or embassy, or by calling the Costa Rican Tourist Board office in Miami, WATS 800-327-7033 from the continental US; (305) 358-2150 from Florida and elsewhere. Address: 200 SE First St., Suite 400, Miami, FL 33131.

As we go to press, the exchange has just been raised to 48 colones per US$1 (Nov. 1984). You can exchange money only at banks, though hotels will exchange some for guests. Penalties for exchanging money otherwise are severe and not worth the risk. The banks will charge a commission to exchange travelers' checks but not cash. You may want to carry some cash (carefully) in US dollars especially for airport taxes, baggage charges, etc., when you may have used up your colones before leaving. Some flights may arrive after banks have closed and you need to pay cab fare to town. You will only be able to cash US$50 back from colones into dollars when you leave, so you may want to have some travelers' checks in small denominations so you come out fairly even. If you will be staying in villages, you should cash some colones into rather small bills, as even a 100 colon note (about $2) can be a problem to break. Major U.S. credit cards can be used for car rentals, excess baggage, and expensive hotels.

Safety

What are you to think when the American press refers to the political and military problems of Guatemala, El Salvador and Nicaragua as "Central America"? At least it's better than the former practice of calling everything between Mexico and Peru "banana republics." Even with the problems to the north, Costa Rica remains peaceful with great determination. Its democracy and neutrality together with lack of an army are its greatest sources of national pride. While residents are concerned about problems to the north, at presstime no one I met felt that there was any chance of CR getting involved.

Paseo Colon, one of the main avenues in San Jose.

There is far less violence in the entire country in a month than there is in any major U.S. city in a night. You are personally at least as safe here as you would be anywhere on earth, including at home.

Theft has always been here and has increased with the economic crisis and the admission of thousands of refugees who have not been able to find work. The bars across ground floor windows of most houses and other buildings will probably startle you on your first drive into San Jose from the airport. The vast majority of the people you see are the most honest people in the world, but here, as elsewhere, there are some of the others— and they are very quick and expert. I always take the precautions listed below.

On my first vacation in Costa Rica I didn't lose a thing and never had an unpleasant incident though I rambled mostly by myself all over the country on foot, in taxis, buses, trains, fishing boats, and once a cattle truck when the bus pulled out suddenly and left me. On the research trip for this book I was careful most of the time. One morning however, I was at the Coca Cola bus terminal in San Jose in one of the worst neighborhoods of the city. I was catching a bus to Santa Rosa National Park and had my backpack and camera pack. I stupidly had my wallet in an outer pocket of the camera pack slung around my neck in front of me. While I wrestled the backpack into the baggage compartment under the bus, someone slipped out the wallet so quickly and carefully that I didn't miss it until I got on the bus. Then I had to cancel the trip as I didn't have any money with me to get back from the park. I had lost $110 in cash and my tourist card, but nothing else as my passport and all other money were at home. I cashed in the bus ticket to get back to the house, much wiser. My suggestions, which apply to travel anywhere:

1. When traveling, always look as neat and clean as humanly possible—but don't look affluent. Lots of jewelry and matched sets of leather luggage may make you feel more important when you arrive at a hotel, but unless you have Princess Diana's security forces, they aren't worth it. At best you are a mark for every cab driver and merchant who can raise his price. At worst you are an easy target for major theft. In particular, gold neck chains with pendants and pierced earrings of any value are likely to be taken off you in the street (with possible damage to neck or ears). I never wear an expensive-looking watch, and keep cameras out of sight unless using them.

2. Try to avoid taking more luggage than you can carry at one time. Besides making travel easier, this saves leaving anything behind when moving through airline and bus terminals. Backpacks are handy, but avoiding a hippy look can save a lot of trouble with customs and unpopularity with villagers.

3. When you are out for day or evening, try to avoid carrying anything you don't need at the time. Hotels can keep your extra money, cameras and other valuables in their safes. In villages I have left my passport and all extra money with the thoroughly honest owner of the cabin I was using. In Costa Rica you will have a tourist card and may or may not have a passport. Since the tourist card has your passport number on it, there is no reason to be carrying your passport, even to cash checks, as long as

you will be coming back to the same hotel. That saved me when my wallet was stolen, as the passport also had the visa stamped in it. Of course passport and credit card numbers should be recorded and kept separately so you have them when reporting a theft. Lately the police have stopped travelers on the street and demanded to see passports. A photocopy of the first several pages of your passport including its number, your photo, and your entry visa stamped at the airport are sufficient at this time. Of course if you plan to stay 30 days or less, you may have only a tourist card.

In summary, don't bring anything you don't really need, try not to carry anything you don't need that day, and watch or have someone else watch anything you put down. These cautions apply as well anywhere you travel and are not unique to Costa Rica.

Cultural Sensitivity

Nowhere in the world are people more helpful, hospitable, and friendly than the Costa Ricans. Most have had enough contact with North Americans (many have lived for years in the United States or elsewhere abroad) to be understanding and to forgive us our gringo differences. When I asked a young Costa Rican how he spoke such accent-free English, he said "Oh, I lived in Los Angeles for 15 years." He made some of the comments and suggestions given here.

Dress—San Jose is more cosmopolitan than elsewhere in the country and slacks on women are acceptable here. You will see young ticas in blue jeans frequently. Do dress up for performances at the National Theater and other occasions important to the Costa Ricans. Wearing blue jeans there doesn't show respect to the people or their culture. For men or women, shorts are for sports and the beach *only*. In villages which may be less liberal, I wear skirts unless I'm going hiking or riding.

All Latin Americans consider themselves as American as citizens of the United States of America. Travelers from the United States can show consideration, and it will be appreciated, if they refer to themselves as "norteamericanos" or North Americans.

Machismo still exists in Latin America but much less in Costa Rica than elsewhere and is much less a problem for foreign women here than in most other places. The most obvious sign I have seen in all my rambling is polite surprise from men and women alike at the weird things gringo women do—travel alone, hike, ride, swim and live alone, fly planes, operate their own boats and businesses, and make all the important decisions in their own lives. When I was camping by myself in Santa Rosa National Park, the mother of a large family swarming around the campground asked "Are you a writer?". Apparently writers

Proud young Costa Rican on Santa Ana street near San Jose.

are forgiven for being even crazier than other tourists and wanting solitude. I have never had an incident involving a Costa Rican despite my often being the only woman present.

A Costa Rican advises "Don't be blatant in manners, dress, or voice. Blend in. The locals catch on quickly if you stand out. Explain clearly (not loudly) what you need and want. Check things said to you for truth." People sometimes want to please you enough to say "si," yes, to anything you ask.

"Single North American girls have a bad reputation, so many men think they're an easy catch. Show that you respect yourself."

Nude bathing is at best completely offensive to Costa Ricans. At worst it's downright dangerous to bathers in some areas and has led to serious incidents. The white sand beach at Cahuita may look like a deserted island to you, but it's these people's front yard and the path behind it through coconut palms is the walkway to their homes. In some coastal villages the local girls are never taught to swim though safety and enjoyment are lost because their parents don't want them exposed to nudity on the beach. What a shame!

Costa Rican men are polite and possibly more considerate than you are used to. One can be a lady or gentleman anywhere. Here you'll find that an interest in the people and their concerns makes your trip more enjoyable and enlightening.

How To Get There

Presently the recommended way to get to Costa Rica is by airline to San Jose (with the exception perhaps of riding a bus north from Panama). Some people drive the Inter–American Highway or ride buses (the TICA buses are comfortable and air conditioned, running down the highway and stopping only at national capitals), with bus riding undoubtedly safer than driving your own vehicle. Until peace returns to Guatemala, El Salvador, and Nicaragua, driving through them isn't safe. If you ride the LACSA (Costa Rican) flight from Los Angeles or the SAHSA (Honduran) flight from New Orleans, you may be surprised to land at San Salvador or Managua briefly en route.

From most US and Canadian points, fares to San Jose are cheapest via Miami (even from San Francisco and Seattle!) as there is more competition to Miami than to the other US departure cities. LACSA, the Costa Rican airline, controls fares to San Jose and the rates with them or any other line flying there are comparatively high. This could change. The flights from New Orleans, Houston, and Los Angeles do offer scenic views of volcanoes and reefs down the Mexican and Central American coasts. The only airlines flying nonstop from Miami to San Jose at presstime are LACSA and Eastern Airlines. Aeronica (Nicaraguan) lands in Managua and SAHSA (Honduran) lands in Tegucigalpa en route.

If you're going for 30 days or less, have your travel agent search carefully for excursion fares or package plans which may involve some nights at designated hotels, but often take a large discount off the regular fare. There are many well-informed travel agents who are willing to make the effort. One who was recommended to me in Costa Rica and whom I have since used successfully is a Honduran in Seattle, Javier Pinel, America's Tours, 1218 3rd Ave., Seattle, WA 98101. (800) 552-7330. He seems to be able to recite Latin American fares from memory on the phone.

Juan Santamaria Airport, Costa Rica's modern jet airport near Alajuela.

The following airlines fly to Costa Rica from Europe, North and South America: For their local addresses, see your travel agent. Their San Jose addresses are given because you'll need to confirm your return flight.

AERONICA
Calle 1 Ave. 2
Tel. 23-02-26/33-24-83

AVIANCA/SAM
Calle 1 Ave. 5
Tel. 30-30-66

COPA
Calle 1 Ave. 5
Tel. 21-55-96, 22-34-01,
22-49-07

IBERIA
Calle 1 Ave 2/4
Tel. 21-33-11
Airport tel. 41-25-91

EASTERN
Calle ctl. Ave. 1/3
Tel. 21-66-13

KLM
Calle 1 Ave ctl./1
Tel. 21-09-22

LACSA
Calle 1 Ave. 5
Tel. 31-05-11
Airport tel. 41-62-44

MEXICANA
Calle 1 Ave. 2/4
Tel. 22-17-11

SANSA (local airline)
Calle 24 Ave. ctl/1
Tel. 21-94-14, 33-03-07

SAHSA
Calle 1/3 Ave. 5
Tel. 21-57-74, 21-55-61

TACA
Calle 2 Ave. 3
Tel. 22-17-90, 22-17-44

Baggage. Most international airlines allow 66 lbs. of baggage. Some weigh your carry-on bag as part of it. You'll be happier if you don't have to carry or look after more than that anyway. SAHSA, for one, charges $1 per pound for excess baggage from New Orleans to San Jose! There's motivation for packing light! Experienced travelers advise you to check your baggage only to your point of departure from your home country and make the transfer to the international airline yourself. It's much easier to cope with lost luggage in Miami than to wonder where it went after you arrive in San Jose. Your luggage should be secure, locked, and not easily slit with a knife. It should be well marked and have your address inside as well. I use laundry marking pen on the luggage itself as well as luggage tags. Your carry-on bag must fit under the seat in front of you. It should contain medicine and any other really indispensables—or irreplaceables. Mine has my address books, cameras, binoculars, film, glasses, bathing suit, and one set of clothes including shoes. Anything else I could replace in San Jose if I had to. Any prescription drugs should be worn under clothing; it's wise not to wear it through customs. A friend was strip-searched in Peru because the authorities had no other way to be assured what she was carrying. You are allowed to take into Costa Rica $100 value in gifts for friends.

You may bring 2 cameras and any reasonable amount of film. If you are doing serious or professional photography and will need more than that, you are advised to take a list of your equipment and serial numbers to the nearest Costa Rican consulate before you leave home. They simply want to be sure you will bring them back with you instead of selling them en route. If your equipment, including watch and binoculars, wasn't made in your home country, you may save some delay on your return by taking the same list and equipment to your own country's nearest customs office for recording (this list is then good for as long as you own the equipment and doesn't have to be redone for each trip).

SANSA DC-3 lands at Golfito airport, surrounded by a golf course. It's an inexpensive half-hour flight from San Jose.

International Flights

LACSA   To/From: Venezuela (Maracaibo, Caracas)
                        Colombia (Baranquilla, Cartagena)
                        Panama, Honduras, Guatemala, Mexico
                        (City, Cancún)
                        U.S. (Los Angeles, Miami, New Orleans)
Eastern   To/From: U.S. (Miami), South American points.
KLM   To/From: Holland, Curacao, Trinidad, Tobago,
                        Portugal
Iberia   To/From: Madrid, Havana, Puerto Rico, Peru
COPA   To/From: Panama, Managua, San Salvador,
                        Guatemala
SAHSA   To/From: Managua, Honduras, Belize, U.S. (New
                        Orleans, Houston)
Aeronica   To/From: Nicaragua, Panama, U.S. (Miami)
Mexicana   To/From: Mexico, Guatemala, U.S. (Los Angeles,
                        Miami)
SAM   To/From: Colombia

Domestic Flights

SANSA   To/From: Quepos, Puerto Limón, Rió Frió. Coto
                        47, Golfito, Liberia, Tamarindo

Farmer leads his oxen along street in Jicaral on Nicoya Peninsula.

Entry & Departure Requirements

While the documentation and procedures vary somewhat depending on your citizenship, the requirements for U.S. citizens given here are fairly typical. To encourage tourism, the entry and exit procedures have been greatly streamlined for visits of 30 days or less. While you can get extensions up to a total of 6 months, the method has not been improved and can take several days of your time if you have to go to Immigration in San Jose.

For visits of 30 days or less, you don't need a passport. You simply take a birth certificate, voter registration card or similar identification to the airline ticket office at your airport of departure from the United States. They will issue you a tourist card, good for 30 days. You must have a round trip or onward ticket showing you will leave Costa Rica. You may be required to show proof of adequate funds. For U.S. citizens, this card is good for more than one entry to Costa Rica during the 30-day period. However if you go to Panama or somewhere else for more than 72 hours, you may want to get another tourist card to reenter Costa Rica as that would give you another 30 days. A visa will be stamped on the tourist card when you enter Costa Rica. Have at least 2 copies of your passport photo with you (it's best to have several extras). For longer stays you do need a passport.

For stays of 30 to 60 days, here are 2 ways to avoid going in person to stand in Immigration's lines: 1. Take your passport to a Costa Rican consulate in the U.S. before you leave and have a 60-day visa stamped in the passport, or 2. Near the end of the first 30 days, but not after it, take your passport, tourist card, 3 passport pictures and your airline ticket out of the country to a travel agent in San Jose and ask him to get you an exit permit which is required if you're in the country over 30 days. Make a copy of the first pages of your passport showing its number, your photo and the entry visa stamp, and carry these pages while the agent uses your passport to get the exit permit. That exit permit, which includes a stamp from the court that you don't owe child support, then gives you an automatic 30 days beyond your original 30 days. At the end of that time you *must* leave Costa Rica for at least 72 hours. The travel agent will charge a small fee for all of this, including the charge for all the revenue stamps required. It is well worth it, as it saves you 2 trips to Immigration and at least half a day's time standing in line. The travel agent or his staff speak English. Many of the people behind Immigration's windows don't, or don't admit it.

If you want to stay more than 60 days and don't want to interrupt your trip by visiting another country, you will have to get your own extension, though you can get a travel agent to get the exit permit for you when you're ready to leave. If you've stayed over 92 days, you'll need a statement from the Ministerio de Haciendo that you don't owe any taxes (see if the travel agent will get that while getting your exit permit).

Having spent 4 precious days of my research trip standing in lines at Immigration, I hope the ICT people trying to cut red tape for tourists will prevail—however it's another government department.

The Immigration offices at Puntarenas and Puerto Limón are supposed to have shorter lines than you'll find in San Jose, especially before holidays. Be sure to bring all the materials mentioned above and enough travelers' checks to show that you have at least $150 for each month you plan to stay. A 90-day extension is the most they'll give at one time, but try to get that instead of 30 or 60 days if it will save you having to come back. Avoid the young fellows in the courtyard who will offer to help (for a price). One took me to the wrong department and cost me a day.

Immigration is in buildings surrounding 2 courtyards across from Parque Nacional on Ave. 1 Calle 19/21. It's open from 8 to 4, Monday through Friday. Get there by 7:15 a.m., early in the week. Go to the window with the sign "Prorrogas de Turismo." Some people in that office do speak English. They'll look at your passport and other documents, have you copy a form in Spanish, and tell you which line to stand in next. Be sure to ask them how much value in revenue stamps you'll need when you get to the head of *that* line. If you go stand in the stamps line now, you can avoid waiting twice in the other line! You will have to surrender your passport for which you'll get a receipt to carry for the several days before they will give back the passport. If you get your own exit visa, you'll also have to go 2 blocks to the

Court Building (Tribunales) and stand in line at the window where they take your passport and check the child support records. The system works, but it's quite a test of patience.

Early Sunday morning fruit and vegetable market in Santa Ana where villagers buy fresh produce directly from the farmers.

Entering Costa Rica

Costa Rica has made entry at the airport as simple and convenient as I've ever seen it. You line up before Immigration's windows just inside the terminal and they check your passport and look in the big book of computer records to see if you've been in trouble here before. If you haven't, you're quickly allowed on past the offices for exchanging money or cashing travelers' checks into colones, and the ICT office which can call hotels downtown to find a room for you. If you use either of these services, your baggage will already be waiting for you in the claim area when you get there. Customs check of your baggage is quick and efficient (perhaps more detailed if you come from cocaine growing countries to the south), and 20 minutes from the time you entered the terminal, you may be climbing the stairs to the street outside! Welcome to Costa Rica!

Outside you'll find cabs, minibuses, car rentals and the bus stop for the San Jose-Alajuela bus just across the driveway. The latter is only a few cents all the way to San Jose but won't take any more than carry-on luggage. It's worth remembering if you ever turn in a rental car at the airport. With tourist luggage, the cheapest way to town is the minibus which will stop at hotels. Airport cabs cost about twice as much per mile as all other cabs in the country and they won't bargain. It's about $8 to town by cab. Enjoy the ride to San Jose on the modern "autopista," turnpike, past coffee plantations, several industrial plants, Hospital Mexico, several deluxe hotels, and the Cariari Country Club. You'll pass Sabana Park as you enter downtown San Jose.

What to Bring

You'll undoubtedly have some items you'd add to this list, but keep it light and leave room for what you may want to bring back. If you select 1 or 2 base colors and make sure everything else goes with them, you'll have a variety of costumes with a limited wardrobe. Cotton is cooler than synthetics, but everything should be wash and wear. I never travel with light-colored slacks, shorts, or skirts as they look grubby after I've sat down twice. I bring a navy lightweight suit with skirt and slacks, a navy denim skirt, field pants and hiking shorts. All blouses are in light colors that go with them. Navy Birkenstock sandals softened the miles of San Jose's stone sidewalks and worked well with a denim skirt for days at a time in buses and jeeps in the countryside. A skirt is far cooler on the coasts than slacks, and should be full enough to allow climbing into bus or boat. Men should bring a lightweight suit and 1 or 2 ties (for travel and evenings in San Jose), plus slacks. As soon as possible you'll want a *guayabera* shirt, the white or cream shirt Latin American men wear open at the neck and not tucked in. It's dressy enough for almost anything and saves wearing ties, etc. to dinner. You don't need coat and tie outside of San Jose. Flowered shirts from Hawaii will mark you a tourist and are suitable only at the beach.

Women:	Men:
1 suit w/skirt & slacks	1 suit
2 skirts (1 denim, 1 print, etc.)	2 dress shirts

3 blouses (1 sleeveless, others short)
1 dressy dress
1 pair slacks
1 pair shorts
1 bathing suit
Sweater or light jacket
3 sets underwear
3 pairs socks, 2 pairs pantyhose
1 pair street shoes (walking)
2 pairs sandals (dressy, walking)
1 pair running or tennis shoes
Manicure set, inexpensive earrings

3 sport shirts
2 pairs slacks
1 pair jeans or equiv.
1 pair shorts
1 pair swimming trunks
Sweater or sport jacket
3 sets underwear
4 pairs socks
1 pair street shoes
1 pair sandals
1 pair running or tennis shoes
Shaving gear

Both Men and Women:
Towel (hotels won't let theirs go to beach)
Washcloth
Universal flat drain cover for wash basin
Sun hat
Sun glasses
Toilet paper (small amount)
Sunscreen (SPF #4 or 6 and SPF #15 or 18)
Insect repellent
Anti-itch ointment
Bandaids
Moleskin
Aspirin
Kaopectate
Pepto Bismol
Toothbrush & paste
Hairbrush & comb
Vitamin pills (optional)
Umbrella, folding. Cheap in San Jose. Essential.

Ear plugs (if you can sleep in them)
Sewing kit
Alarm clock
Flashlight

According to your special interests:
Fins, mask snorkel
Day pack
Sleeping or bivouac bag
Canteen & water drops
Pocket knife
Cup, spoon, bowl
Binoculars
Photography gear
Battery-powered fan
Hiking boots
Goretex parka, pants
Pile jacket
Stocking cap
Malaria pills

If you plan to spend many nights in the discos of San Jose, or you're a field biologist or in the Peace Corps, your interests will affect your choices.

Time

Costa Rica is on Central Standard Time, 6 hours behind Greenwich Mean Time. Since it's as far east as Miami, in the Eastern Time Zone, the sun comes up around 6 a.m. all year and sets in early evening. The whole country seems to get an early start to its day.

Street in Puerto Limón.

Telephones

You can dial direct between Costa Rica and most other countries, keeping track of time zones. It's more expensive to dial from Costa Rica to the US than in the other direction, especially if you use the low cost times of day. The access numbers for Costa Rica are 011-506 plus the number. From Costa Rica to the US, dial 116 plus the number. Within Costa Rica there are some villages with just 1 phone number with or without an exchange and extensions, e.g. Cahuita and Puerto Viejo. Many hotels on the coasts do have a San Jose number. This can be the easiest way to make reservations for lower-priced hotels which don't have foreign representatives. Generally if you want reservations in hotels that cost less than $10/night, you'll need to speak Spanish.

Pay phones in San Jose seem to be on busy corners with loud diesel trucks shifting gears. Costa Rican coins come in old, new, and newer denominations, and the phone you're facing usually takes coins you don't have. Passersby will help if they can. Use their help or find a phone inside somewhere.

Many foreigners who've moved into Costa Rica haven't been able to get phones in their own names so the phones are listed in someone else's, effectively making them unlisted. Be sure you have your friends' numbers as you won't be able to look them up.

Addresses

Practically all Costa Rican mailing addresses are "Apartados," abbreviated "Apdo.", meaning post office box. Street numbers don't exist or aren't used. Neither are street names outside of San Jose. All directions are given in meters or varas (33 inches) from something else which may not still be there. The tree was cut down or the Coca Cola bottling plant is long gone, but everyone knows where it was! I lived in a very nice house in a good suburb of San Jose, but the address was (in Spanish of course) "225 meters south and 100 meters west of the church, near the brown garbage container." Don't try it in the dark the first time, especially from a bus and bus stop you don't know. A taxi driver might be able to find it. A friend who had to pick me up was smart enough to ask whether those directions were from the front or back of the big church. You may want a compass as well as some patience.

Mail

Air mail takes about 5 days each way between Costa Rica and the US or Canada, the same to Europe. Surface mail takes weeks. If you're sending mail from Costa Rica, mail it at your hotel desk or a *main* post office, for reliability, and don't put anything but a letter in it. Mail to you should be sent in care of your hotel or to you at "Lista De Correos," general delivery. Zip or postal codes are put before the name of the town, e.g. 1000 San Jose. Do underline both Costa Rica and Central America on the envelope, in hopes the postal clerks won't send it to Puerto Rico!

Try not to have anyone send you anything but letters. Other items go to customs warehouses, often in another town, and the duty can be very high, with no relation to the value of the item. Getting there at the right time to pick it up can be a big nuisance. Even personal photographs or cassette tapes with messages on them aren't worth it. The same applies to packages you might want to send Costa Rican friends after you get home. Don't do it. They might have to pay $15 in duty and spend half a day to pick up a $5 present. Perhaps you can find a friend visiting Costa Rica who won't mind taking something small in the $100 in gifts a traveler can bring.

Modern highway bridge on the freeway (autopista) near San Jose. (ICT)

Getting Around

Public transportation within the country is subsidized and is very reasonable.

Air SANSA is the airline within Costa Rica with daily prop plane flights between San Jose and Puerto Limón, Liberia, Tamarindo, Quepos, Golfito, and Coto 47 near the Panamanian border. Most fares are under $20 and the flights are about half an hour.

Trains We've discussed the train to Limón and the electric train to Pantarenas, both recommended scenic rides, at minimal cost. The Northern Railway which runs to Limón also has shorter runs to Alajuela and Heredia. Check with the train station at Ave. 3 Calle 17/19 or the ICT for schedules. A banana train runs between Golfito and Palmar daily. It carries passengers on Sundays, an interesting jaunt if you're staying in Golfito then. In San Jose, while the tracks connect the two stations, the station for the Pacific train is in the southwest corner of town at Ave. 20 Calle 2. The Pacific train leaves several times a day.

Buses Costa Ricans ride buses to go anywhere. If there's a road, there's probably a bus, though it may not be daily. Buses on main highways to Golfito, Puerto Limón, Puntarenas, and Liberia are very comfortable. Fares are low—$3 will take you a long distance. The bus from San Jose to Golfito takes about 7 hours, including a lunch stop, and follows the Inter-American Highway from Cartago south over the summit of Cerro de la Muerte, over 11,000 ft. If it's clear, you have glimpses of both the Atlantic and Pacific Oceans as the road winds along the backbone of the Talamanca Range. It drops down to the Valle de General across a slope where landslides during the rainy season sometimes do block it, and reaches Golfito in mid-afternoon, for about $3.75 US! There is no central bus station in San Jose, though buses to the north and west leave from the site or neighborhood of the former Coca Cola bottling plant, Ave. 3 Calle 16/18. You'll have to ask where the bus to _____ stops, as it may be anywhere within a block or two of the center. Buses to Golfito leave from the station across from the Pacifico train station (very early in the morning), Ave. 20 Calle 2. Buses to Cartago and Turrialba leave from Calle 13 Ave. ctl./2. Buses to Puerto Limón leave from Ave. 3 Calle 15/17.

If you're going to ride buses often, some Spanish is essential for at least one member of your party. You do have to be able to ask and receive directions and schedules. Around tourist hotels someone always speaks English. In and around public buses they don't necessarily. You don't need very much, however, if you're polite and prepared for some confusion. Be careful of your possessions, especially around the San Jose stations, and don't show much money when buying tickets. Try to carry as little luggage as possible. Some buses have storage below, but local buses don't, and backpacks or large suitcases don't fit on the overhead racks inside.

Taxis Taxis are quite inexpensive, except for the airport cabs. None have meters, and fares are a matter of bargaining—the more Spanish the better. You should agree on the fare before getting into the cab. Fares can vary according to the time of day, the driver's attitude, yours, how affluent you look (don't expect to bargain about 30 colones with a Nikon hanging around your neck!), and whether you're going or coming from an expensive hotel. My mail was held at a friend's office in the Playboy Hotel. I soon learned to save 40 colones every trip by naming the nearest street intersection instead of the hotel when agreeing on

Rio Colorado Lodge and the tour boat that serves the inland waterway from Moin to Barra Colorado.

74

the fare, though I could later direct the cab to the door. You can ask several drivers to reach a consensus. Some hotel desks are good sources of advice, while those at deluxe hotels may add a bit. The ICT office under the Cultural Plaza may tell you the going rate is something like 30 colones for the first kilometer and 5 or 10 for each additional.

In outlying areas some cabs are 4-wheel drive. Particularly if there are several in your party, it may be practical to hire a cab and driver for the day for some trips, e.g. from Puerto Limón to Cahuita or Puerto Viejo and back. They'll add a bit for the state of the road, but it may save you hours of waiting for a bus to come back. Taxi drivers are not tipped.

Tours Tours are increasing throughout Costa Rica, although practically all are still based in San Jose. There are multi day tours to the more remote national parks, Barra Colorado, Tortuguero, Monteverde, and the Nicoya Peninsula. There are many day tours in and around San Jose, mostly in minivans. They pick you up and drop you off at your hotel, and you may be able to visit several sites in one day, e.g. Irazú and the Orosí Valley. The driver speaks English and any other languages required. He'll tell you about what you're passing en route to the main object. You spend your time sightseeing instead of waiting in bus stations or perhaps riding crowded buses, and the vans are clean and comfortable. You pay for the extra service and you don't meet Costa Ricans except for your driver. Tour drivers are tipped.

The tours I have been on have been excellent, even to places I have also reached by public bus such as Irazú and Poás. There are nature and other special interest tours. The *One Day Adventure Tours* are a cooperative effort by **Calypso Tours**, with boat tours in the Gulf of Nicoya; **Finca Obladi-Oblada**, with horseback nature rides; and **Costa Rica Expeditions**, rafting on the Reventazón River. All of them are well done and fun. Tours on the train use the newly refurbished cars with comfortable seats, restaurant and bar. The tour operators who contributed to that cost have priority in reserving that space which may or may not be available to the independent traveler. More tours and operators are being added to the list you'll find at the back of this book.

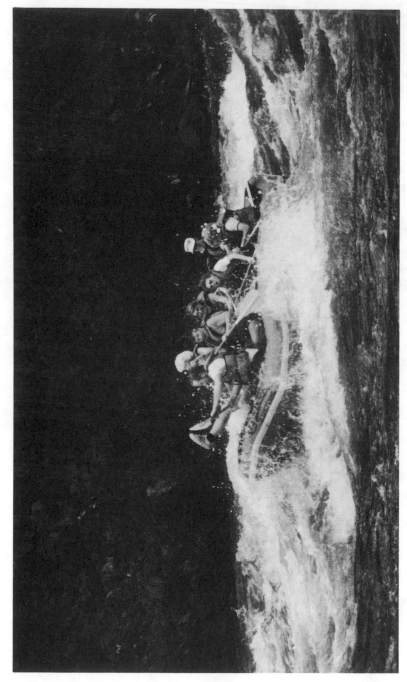

Travelers, including the author right rear, enjoy rafting rapids on the Reventazón River on a day tour from San Jose with Costa Rica Expeditions. (Tom Stultz, Whetstone Photography)

Car rental This isn't something to jump into as lightly as you might at home. Costa Rica has one of the world's highest per capita accident rates. Passing on the narrow two-lane (or less) roads is a very macho competitive sport. Try Sunday afternoon on the highway above Esparza with the crowd returning from a weekend at the beach competing with buses and loaded cattle trucks heading for Monday market in San Jose. On the winding, steep grade buses and trucks pass in both directions. San Jose streets are one way and narrow with almost no parking except lots and garages.

There are freeways for some miles near San Jose. Cars shouldn't be left overnight except in a fenced area. In daylight all baggage should be stowed out of sight in the trunk. I can think of few things that would persuade me to drive in San Jose at all. Cars in Costa Rica don't have heaters or defrosters, though the controls may be there. They don't need heaters, but do need defrosters in the rain (you need a rag to wipe with). Prices for rentals are similar to those in the United States, though gas is over $2 US per gallon. International rental chains will take major credit cards.

Car Rentals

Accion Rent a Car
Sabana Norte
Phone 32-96-37

Avis Rent a Car
Calle 36, Ave. 7
Phone 22-60-66

Budget Rent a Car
Calle 30, Paseo Colón
Phone 23-32-84

Dollar Rent a Car
Calle ctl., Ave. 9
Phone 33-33-39

El Indio Rent a Car
Calle 40/42, Ave. ctl.
Phone 33-21-57

Elegante Rent a Car
Calle 10, Ave. 13/15
Phone 22-89-20

National Car Rental
Calle 30, Paso Colón
Phone 33-44-06

Tico Rental Cars S.A.
Calle 10, Ave. 13/15
Phone 21-01-36

Toyota Rent a Car
Calle 36, Ave. 7
Phone 23-22-50

When the sign says "doble tracción solamente" (4-wheel drive only), believe it!

Your valid driver's license is good for 3 months in Costa Rica. After that you need to get one there. Insurance is a state monopoly and you can get it through the car rental agency. Rental agencies in the San Jose area are listed below. Note that most are on the west side of downtown San Jose or at the airport, or both.

For a higher rate, some have 4-wheel drive vehicles. Be sure that's what you need before spending the extra money for a vehicle that's less comfortable for any number of people over two. Most of the popular beaches can be reached by ordinary cars. Ask about road conditions. If you're spending a week at a resort, it may not make sense to have a rental car parked there costing money when there's usually some cheaper, less worrisome way to get there.

If you do have an accident, don't move the vehicles until the police make out a report. Note the traffic police numbers below.

I rented the smallest possible Toyota from Budget for a 3-day research swing through Puntarenas, Jaco Beach, Quepos and Manuel Antonio from San Jose. I couldn't have covered the ground with all the stops I needed any other way. Everything went well. The car cost $140 US, including the fuel I bought. The cost may seem more reasonable if there are several of you.

Traffic Police

San Jose	22-43-05, 23-80-45, 22-10-05
Alajuela	41-62-08
Cartago	51-90-64
Heredia	37-04-38
Liberia	66-04-09
Limon	58-11-48
Puntarenas	61-03-40

Driving in Costa Rica requires more concentration than I usually give it at home, even on the freeways near San Jose. On the back roads you are advised to "drive like a bullfighter," as one friend said, demonstrating how he passed around holes in the road. Save wear and tear on vehicle and passengers by slowing and shifting as necessary for bumps. Unlit livestock, holes, and pedestrians make driving at night something to avoid. If you find fresh branches lying in the road, it means someone has car trouble just ahead.

Service stations are far apart, and many villages have none. You should fill up in main towns like Liberia, Santa Cruz, or Nicoya before heading to beach resorts. These also may be the only places you can get tire or other repairs.

Hitchhiking On back roads you'll meet people trying to get a ride to town because there isn't a bus until tomorrow or the next day. I'm not sure how successful they are on roads with little traffic, but you may not be able to count on it anywhere in the country. With bus fare so cheap, that's the way to go if there's a bus. Otherwise it's worth asking and trying to find someone going the same way.

Maps Maps to help you get around are free or inexpensive everywhere. ICT and your hotel can furnish maps of downtown San Jose and simple resort maps of the country. Car rental agencies give out road maps, though no one seems to have one with most of the smaller roads, and of course none tells you which streams have bridges. The stationers/bookstores, Libreria Lehmann, Ave. ctl, Calle 1/3, and Libreria Universal, Ave. ctl, Calle ctl/1, have good map sections. At Lehmann's I found the aeronautical chart of Costa Rica. At a scale of 1:500,000, it's a great map to bring back to show your friends where you've been as it shows all the mountains in shaded relief so you can see the shape of the country. It's about 2½ by 3½ feet, a fine, inexpensive souvenir. They also have smaller maps that show just about anything. The Ministry of Transport, Ave. 18, Calle 9, has topographic maps and street maps of towns.

Hotel Comments

Hotels in each town are described as I found them, either on inspection or by staying in them. Some, inspected at quiet midday, may prove to have a cantina operating loudly at night in the block behind. A change of owner or manager could make a large difference for better or worse in cleanliness or service. I welcome comments based on your experience.

Costa Rica has over 300 hotels, some luxurious and some basic where farm workers stay when they come to town on weekends. In between are many inexpensive to moderate hotels with very considerate staffs. You can decide not only what you're willing to pay, but how much luxury you want. Do you want to stay in a "tipico" hotel, where you feel the character of the country and some of your fellow residents are Costa Rican, or do you want to relax in the same atmosphere you'd find in Hawaii or Palm Springs? Or would you like some of each for variety?

For this book I inspected (with a checklist) over 160 hotels all over the country, priced from $.75 to $150 per night, single. I looked at almost all the moderate to luxurious hotels, missing only a handful that operated in late 1983. However, when I found clean hotels in good neighborhoods for less than $3 single, I felt I could do more for you than spend days wandering by myself through the red light districts of San Jose and Puerto Limón inspecting the cheap ones there. If you want these, many are listed in *The South America Handbook* and *South America On a Shoestring* chapters on Costa Rica.

Costa Rica has many small hotels with a dozen rooms or less, often far from major towns. Most hotels in San Jose or the surrounding hills don't have air conditioning as it's cool at that altitude. On the coasts most travelers from temperate climates will want at least a fan or a building that is built to catch every breeze. On the coast, many inexpensive places don't have hot water, but the tap water is luke warm. Hotels rated inexpensive and higher generally will cash travelers' checks though the exchange rate will not be as good as the bank's, but it's a real help when there is no bank in a resort town. They will often take major credit cards. Some of them have reservation agents abroad whom your travel agent can call free. Without these, you'll have to make your own reservations or get help from the ICT office in the airport when you arrive (they called for me and made the reservations before I cleared customs). The hotels generally have someone behind the desk who speaks English. Often there are local tour representatives in the lobby with whom you can book sightseeing tours.

The Gran Hotel Costa Rica overlooks a plaza with crafts vendors and the National Theater.

In less expensive hotels, you're likely to be more on your own if your Spanish is limited, though the manager will often go to amazing lengths to help you. On the East Coast practically all the blacks speak English. You may have a choice between rooms with and without bath. You should inspect rooms in really basic hotels before checking in to see if they're what you want. Everyone has his own definition of basic.

If you make reservations, you should make every effort to keep them or to cancel well ahead. A hotel with very few rooms may have turned away business to hold your reservation, put on extra staff, or laid in more food. This is especially important for groups, but should be done by individuals as well.

The hotels are listed for each town later in this book. The exchange rate at the time was 42.10 colones/$1 US. Since then the colon has been devalued slightly and is expected to drop further. Expensive hotels give their prices in dollars which they don't decrease with changes in the exchange rate. None of the prices here include the 13% tourist and sales tax charged nationally or any service charge. Inflation will cause some rates to rise, but probably not greatly as long as tourism is depressed due to tensions in the nations north of Costa Rica. Some hotels have no rate for singles and simply charge a rate for the room. Some coastal hotels include meals with the rate, and may have a high season rate for December through March. These ranges are based on the minimum charge for singles and prices go higher for deluxe features. For the current exchange rate when you travel, you can call the nearest Costa Rican embassy or consulate or call the ICT office in Miami toll-free from the continental US, 1-800-327-7033.

Luxury	Over $52/day	Range A
Expensive	$36-52	B
Moderate	$24-36	C
Inexpensive	$13-24	D
Budget	$7-13	E
Basic	up to $7	F

This scale refers to price for a single room in U.S. dollars only and does not refer to features of the hotel which may include a swimming pool in the budget range. A room or cabin for 4 may be a real bargain for a group or family even if it's not for a single.

Couples should ask for their preference in twin or double beds when making reservations. Hotels often have rooms with either.

"Apartotels" and "cabinas" are terms you'll see often. An apartotel has rooms with kitchen facilities, often suites, and usually has weekly and monthly as well as daily rates. There are several in the San Jose area and a few elsewhere. They can be economical for families and very convenient if one is following a diet. Cabina means cabin but is used very loosely by the owners and occasionally even means a room in a multi-story building. Usually, if not cabin, it refers to motel-style ground level rooms. A pension is an inexpensive to basic hotel which usually does not serve meals even if it formerly did.

83

Hotel Tioga in Puntarenas.

Camping

Camping at beaches and national parks is a practical way to stay. Sometimes the nearest hotel is 40 miles away. There are few commercial camping areas, e.g. Jaco Beach south end, and others where it's acceptable as long as you're not in someone's yard or field without permission. If you're camping high in the mountains, as on Rincon de la Vieja, you'll need a good sleeping bag and tent, though sometimes there are shelters or huts. For low-altitude camping here in the tropics, I've found my 18-ounce bivouac bag with a foam sleeping pad for comfort works well. In rain I'd want a plastic sheet overhead. The bivouac bag zips closed with a bug net panel, and I think I could sleep on an ant hill. Avoid grassy stock pastures, which usually have chiggers and ticks.

I used the grassy, tree-shaded campground at Santa Rosa park two nights. The first night I was concerned about crawling creatures and tried sleeping on a picnic table. Unfortunately it had a loose plank on one side and at midnight it dumped me. Falling off a table while zipped up in a bivvy bag is a very helpless feeling! Peace ended at 4 a.m. when a family of howler monkeys on one side of camp joined a chorus of coyotes in the next field.

A hammock is the ideal tropical camp bed for those whose backs will tolerate one.

Camping is the only way to be on hand for turtle nesting or hatching on west coast beaches, and in such unpopulated places, keeping supplied with food and reliable water is your only concern. In settled areas, such as Manuel Antonio, camping is beautiful except during holiday crowds. There are more camping areas being added at beaches like Doña Ana near Puntarenas and at Moin on the Caribbean. Watching your gear or finding someone else to watch it is a problem if you're alone or in a small group and want to leave camp. At Manuel Antonio the ranger station does keep gear for people. I've sometimes stayed in hotel or cabina simply to have a place to leave gear. ICT is working on the problem, but presently your best bet is to camp with others so someone is in the area. Putting your name with permanent laundry marker on your gear to destroy its resale value may help.

There are RV parks along the Inter-American Highway and near San Jose and Heredia. When driving down the highway to Costa Rica again becomes safe, I'll go into detail on them in later editions.

Food

While I've met travelers who can remember after two weeks in New Guinea which night the meat was tough, I'm not one of them. If food is one of your real interests as a traveler, you'll have fun exploring the well-advertised restaurants of every nation in San Jose. For inexpensive meals, small places called *sodas* will serve good plain food for a dollar or so for lunch. The best ice cream in Costa Rica is at the *Pops* chain. *Refrescas* are delightful drinks made with tropical fruits such as mangos and papayas blended with water or milk. *Gallo pinto* is a rice and bean dish that Costa Ricans eat for breakfast and at other meals as well. Shrimp and fish dishes are excellent, and steak is good and very inexpensive. Hotels where I've enjoyed the food will be mentioned in their individual comments. Otherwise, the two restaurants noted are excellent, cheap, and in places you might not easily find, one near Manuel Antonio and one in Santa Cruz. For the environmentally conscious, a note—tortuga (sea turtle) eggs are served in some bars, and the meat is served in restaurants in Limón. All species are endangered and taking eggs or meat is illegal. It probably will continue as long as people maintain the market by buying them.

Costa Ricans enjoy their beaches and throng to the ones reached by bus or good roads.

Health

Costa Rica is the cleanest, most healthful, tropical country I've visited. The people and government are concerned about health and have spent heavily on water supplies, hospitals, and health programs. You can safely drink the water in San Jose and all other major towns, as well as all licensed tourist hotels in outlying areas. In really basic places with their own wells or at roadside pulperias, you may want to stick to soda drinks from the bottle, etc. I carry and use water purification drops when I'm refilling my canteen from streams or wells on camping trips.

86

Food. Milk is pasteurized and market stalls in community markets are incredibly clean. Fish stalls in San Jose, 70+ miles from the sea, don't even smell fishy! In choosing restaurants, I don't take any more care than I would traveling in the U.S., and I haven't been sick despite eating in a wide variety of places all over the country. If you buy fried food from streetside stalls, or vendors on buses and trains, or eat salads in doubtful-looking places, you're on your own. Washing your hands and the pocket knife you may be using to peel fruit before eating is important.

Hikers and campers will probably want to bring insect repellent, though I have only used it a few times in Costa Rica. Note that "deet," the active ingredient in many repellents, makes many people more sensitive to sun. You can use Avon bath oil instead! If you walk across lowland cattle pastures you may encounter chiggers, an almost invisible mite, also found in the southern U.S., whose bite raises welts with a fierce itch that lasts some days. Staying on trails and roads is the best prevention. Being completely covered around the ankles, etc. and changing clothes immediately afterward helps. It's worth carrying a soothing anti-itch lotion. Some people take an antihistamine before bedtime to reduce swelling and itching if they've been bitten.

If you camp or stay in primitive quarters, it's best to hang up all clothing and shake out shoes and clothes before putting them on.

Fer-de-lance, a very poisonous and aggressive snake, on the laboratory floor at Coronado.

Snakes. Except for the Arctic, most areas of the world have poisonous snakes. Despite looking carefully anytime I step off a trail or put my hand up to a tree, I have only seen poisonous snakes in the laboratory in Costa Rica (the non-poisonous boa constrictor in a national park doesn't count). However, I will keep looking for the fer-de-lance (called terciapelo or velvet snake here) which is highly poisonous and very aggressive, the coral snake, water moccasin, etc. In urban areas they aren't a problem. In rural places or wilderness, watch where you are walking. If you want to see them safely, visit the snake lab in Coronado, a northeastern suburb of San Jose, and watch them milked for venom weekday afternoons at 2, from behind a plate glass window.

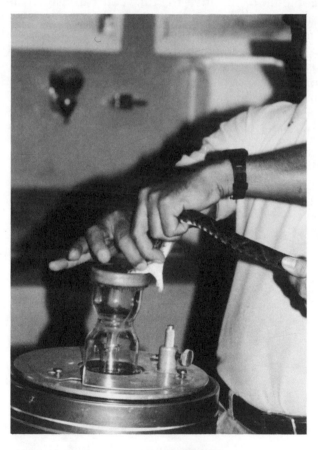

Fer-de-lance donates venom for making anti-venin at Coronado snake lab.

Medical Care. Costa Rica has excellent doctors and hospitals, with the majority in the San Jose area. All hospitals have English-speaking staff members with many doctors having trained in the U.S. or England. For emergency care, go to the hospitals or clinics. For other care, your consulate can provide a list of private doctors. Check with your health insurance before you leave home to see if you need additional coverage or forms.

Immunizations. There are none required or listed as recommended for Costa Rica. If you're staying in major hotels and not camping out or snorkeling, that's fine. If you will be hiking or camping, or spending time near Costa Rica's borders which might not be recognized as barriers by germs and mosquitoes, you may want to take some of the precautions you would for other tropical areas. A gamma globulin shot makes you more resistant to many viruses, including hepatitis, for up to 6 months. Tetanus is a good shot for any outdoor person to keep current. Costa Rica eliminated malaria some years ago, but refugees have recently arrived with some cases. A weekly pill prescribed by your doctor to be taken for several weeks before, during, and after the trip is simple to take if you will be near the borders or going to any other tropical countries on the same trip. No immunizations are required for entry to the United States. Carrying a copy of your immunization records and prescriptions is sensible when traveling.

Sunburn. Ten degrees north of the equator the sun's effect on unprotected skin is serious. A burn from one day in the sun can spoil the next several days of your trip. Long-term exposure can, besides giving you a tan, age your skin drastically. I don't think the leather look has improved the appearance of anyone since Sitting Bull. Fortunately you can avoid this and still go home with a healthy glow.

Using shade where available, a sunscreen lotion, a sun hat, and discretion with the midday sun and length of exposure are sensible. Here you will tan through a thin shirt or while lying in the shade near a beach. Bring effective sunscreens containing PABA. They are labeled now with sun protection factors (SPF), supposed to indicate how much longer an average person can stay out without burning. You will not be in average conditions. As a blonde who does tan well, I use creams with an SPF of 4 or 6 for daytime moisturizers even in the Central Valley. On the beach or outdoors, I use gels with SPFs of 15, the highest generally available. These have names like Block Out and Total Eclipse! Bullfrog is a waterproof sunscreen, SPF 18, highly recommended by raft trip leaders, available at REI stores in the western U.S. In the tropics you will tan through them. It's important to put more on after swimming and every 3 to 4 hours even if you aren't swimming.

Insects, etc. Any tropical area has more insects than you usually see in temperate climates. A biology professor once told my class that the reptiles had their age, the mammals are having theirs now, but he felt that the next would belong to arthropods (insects and all others with jointed legs). If you travel in the tropics you may feel that the insects have always had the upper hand. In warm damp climates they flourish. If you see ants or an occasional cockroach in an otherwise clean establishment, it is not a sign of filth but only means no one has mopped there in the past few minutes. Relax and enjoy the fantastic array of butterflies, moths, and caterpillars that brighten garden and forest here.

HOSPITALS, SAN JOSE	Address	Telephone
Clinica Americana	Calle ctl./1, Ave. 14	22-10-10
Clinica Biblica	Calle ctl./1, Ave. 14	23-64-22
Clinica Catolica	Guadelupe	25-50-55
Clinica Santa Rita (Maternity)	Ave. 8, Calle 15/17	21-64-33
Calderon Guardia	Ave. 9, Calle 17	22-41-33
Children's Hospital	Paseo Colón, Calle 20	22-01-22
Hospital Mexico	Autopista General Cañas	32-61-22
San Juan de Dios (Free emergency service)	Paseo Colón, Calle 14	22-01-66
Red Cross (Ambulance)		21-58-18

HOSPITALS, OTHER CITIES	Telephone	Telephone, Red Cross (Ambulance)
Alajuela	41-50-11	41-29-39
Cartago	51-06-11	51-04-21
Heredia	37-10-91	37-11-15
Liberia	66-00-11	66-09-94
Limón	58-22-22	58-01-25
Puntarenas	63-00-33	61-01-84

Clinicas are private hospitals, available to foreigners at reasonable rates. Others are social security hospitals which provide emergency services to foreigners. All have laboratories, x-rays, and pharmacies.

The tropical jungle has many species, even in a small area overhanging the canal. A green filter on your lens makes them stand out even on black and white film.

Photography

Costa Rica is a great place for photography, whether you're a professional or just carry an Instamatic. The tropical flowers and blossoming trees, wildlife, and constantly changing scenery offer more choices than you'll be able to film in one trip.

Those who've traveled with a camera in the tropics before know what they want to do. For those who haven't, here are a few suggestions:

For any trip, take time to know your camera well before you leave home. If it's new or borrowed, load and shoot some film and get it back to study before you start this trip. Read the manual and practice. Bring all the film you think you'll need for the trip, plus a bit more. Bring extra batteries for your camera and flash, and get silica gel to store with your film to keep it dry. Radio and electronic stores at home receive many stock items packed with it and may be able to give you some. Get lead-foil envelopes made for taking film through airport security—but then carry all your film in your carry-on bag and ask that it be hand-checked instead of x-rayed.

You are allowed to bring 2 cameras and any reasonable amount of film into Costa Rica, but should get your equipment list with serial numbers reviewed by a Costa Rican consulate at home if you want to bring more cameras. Film is very expensive, 2 or 3 times what you pay at home. If you have to buy extra film during the trip, get it from a busy photo store like the IFSA store on Ave. Central across from the Cultural Plaza, where they sell enough so any film they have is fresh. Color film is very sensitive to heat. I leave any I won't need on a coastal trip back with my baggage in San Jose. Both color and black and white soften in high humidity. They may jam the film winding mechanism of your camera or their sprocket holes may break so they won't wind at all. Keep the film in its original cans in a sealed bag with silica gel. I store my film, exposed and unexposed, in a metal ice cream tin with a top and dry the silica gel weekly in an oven. I bring the exposed film back from a trip of 3 months or less and have it processed at home.

Electronic cameras are delicate creatures in the humid, salty air on the coasts. A small amount of corrosion forming on any contacts can stop them for the trip. Keep your cameras as dry as possible and wipe them off before storing even for the night. If

Seventeen turtles crowd this log in the sun!

possible, bring at least 1 backup camera, preferably not a super miniature whose parts are tiny and extra fragile. If you should have to get a camera reparied, you will be lucky if parts are available. The IFSA store can send you to the repair place they use. Note that batteries are considered accessories and your camera may be returned without them if you don't make the person writing the receipt list them.

I use 2 Pentax ME bodies, 1 loaded with black and white (Ilford FP-4) and the other with color (Kodachrome 64, though I bring a few rolls of faster film for forest interiors). The lenses I switch as needed are a Vivitar Series I Macro-Zoom 70-210 mm, a Pentax 50 mm, and a Tokina 28mm. The wide angle lens is good for buildings inside and outside when streets are narrow. It will show the rim and bottom of a volcano when you're standing on it, and is good for getting a whole tree when you're standing in the forest. Both cameras stopped on one trip, one repairable and the other not during the trip. I took a repairman's advice and bought a Pentax K-1000 body when I got back. It's an older, larger, heavier model that takes the same lenses and isn't as automated, but it's much more rugged with fewer electronics to corrode. Now I carry all 3 cameras on trips.

I used a flash often to fill in shadows or get more light in the forest. A tripod or monopod is useful. I used filters to protect the lenses as well as correct light—yellow or green for B-W film and skylight or ultraviolet for color. If you're using fast film, you'll want a neutral density filter to cut tropical midday sun.

If the sky is overcast, a camera with automatic exposure will pick up so much light from the sky that it underexposes everything else. If you set the meter for double the light, the picture subjects will come out. When the sky is blue and you don't have glare off the sea, the automatic camera is fairly accurate. In the forest, it's wise to use a separate light meter.

I carry my cameras in my camera bag securely zipped rather than around my neck when I'm using them, and leave the bag at the hotel desk if I don't need them that day. On the streets of San Jose, Puntarenas, or Puerto Limón, you should be careful of your camera bag (or have a companion watch it) while you take pictures or load film.

Artist painting wood plaque in Sarchí oxcart factory. (ICT)

Arts, Crafts, Souvenirs

Costa Rican craftsmen make beautiful pieces from metal,
leather, ceramics and tropical hardwoods. Artists paint designs
derived from the Moors who invaded Spain on oxcarts such a
those that used to haul coffee to Puntarenas and still work on
back roads. In modern times they paint the designs on trays,
wall placques, and oxcarts from toy size to barbecue stands. You
can watch them do it at small factories in Sarchí, near San Jose.
Many tours as well as the public buses go there. All wooden
crafts are generally less expensive there than in San Jose, though
you can find any crafts in San Jose gift shops. Plain wooden
trays, lamps, candlesticks, etc. show off the grain of exotic tropical hardwoods. Beautiful chairs, tables, beds, and other furniture
are made from the same woods. You may want to see if the shop
can ship something home for you.

94

Oxcart and other samples of the decorative art in Sarchí. Designs are derived from Arabic patterns brought by Moors to Spain and are painted freehand.

Sarchí factory showroom with furniture in exotic hardwoods and decorated oxcarts in all sizes, from toys up.

The San Jose suburb of Moravia is best known for leather crafts including wallets, purses, briefcases, and belts. Leather is comparatively expensive as it's one of Costa Rica's exports.

Many gift shops have gift packs of Costa Rican coffee and the liquor departments in supermarkets (supermercados) have bottles of Cafe Rica, a coffee liqueur like kahlua.

San Jose has many art galleries with original works and prints by Costa Rican artists. Exploring the galleries is fun and some of the work is very impressive.

A Costa Rican I asked said one could bargain anywhere, even in department stores. That may be possible if one looks native and speaks excellent Spanish. You might try it in the central market stalls, and you definitely should bargain with cab drivers. In most stores the prices are fixed.

The central markets with individual stalls selling anything from cheese to birdcages are an experience. The ones in San Jose and Alajuela are especially interesting. One useful item you'll find is the shopping bag made from rice sacks that Costa Rican housewives use to carry purchases home. The bag is large, very strong, and is white or has the rice brand label and design on it. It costs less than a dollar and folds up to nothing in your purse, but is very handy in Costa Rica and back home for shopping and mail. You've probably already gotten that absolute essential, a paragua (umbrella), but if you haven't, it's an excuse for some shopping. Downtown shops and the market stalls have folding ones made in Panama for $5 or less.

Returning Home—Customs

Most countries will not allow you to bring home birds, animals, or plants without a great deal of extra paperwork or permits. Some are prohibited outright, especially live endangered species or products from them. In Costa Rica there are sometimes items made from alligators or jaguar or margay skins. These would be confiscated by customs at your port of entry if you should get that far with them. It's best to buy your orchid plants at home. If you've read this book, you probably have sense enough not to carry drugs across borders. Flights coming from Central or South America into almost any other country are particularly searched. A Labrador retriever worked the baggage carousel diligently in New Orleans when I returned from Costa Rica recently.

There's lots you can bring, much more than your airline baggage allowance. You'll save time at the airport of entry by putting all your purchases and receipts for any expensive items together in one bag. Canadians absent from Canada for more than 7 days are allowed to bring in duty free $150 per year in value plus 40 ounces of liquor. Canada Customs publishes a useful brochure, "I Declare," that's worth studying.

United States citizens who've been abroad for 48 hours or more are allowed a value of $400 each, no matter what age. One quart of alcohol may be included if you're of age and the state you enter allows it. Useful pamphlets are "Your Trip Abroad" from the United States Dept. of State, Washington, D.C., 20520 and "GSP and the Traveler," from the Department of the Treasury, U.S. Customs Service, Washington, D.C. 20229. The latter explains the Generalized System of Preferences, which is a list of 2500 products from developing countries, including Costa Rica, which are allowed into the United States duty free. Wood and metal furniture, but not wicker or straw, is on the list. So are some leather products.

LIVING IN COSTA RICA

Costa Rica encourages foreigners with a guaranteed pension income of at least $300 per month to become "pensionados," living in the country with all the privileges of a citizen except the right to vote and to work for hire (you can with a permit start a business which would hire locals). The intent of the law is to bring money into Costa Rica and to bring people with education and skills from whom Costa Ricans can learn. Thousands of people from many nations, including several thousand from North America, presently live in Costa Rica in any of several resident statuses. Some are having a wonderful time, enjoying the friendly people, climate, low cost of living, and a new chapter in their lives. Others are like the retired aerospace engineer I met at the theater who has used his slightly impaired hearing as an excuse not to learn Spanish and who now spends his days in

Sunday art show by local artists in Parque Morazán.

his apartotel watching TV. He hasn't thought to walk over to the university and volunteer to teach a physics or engineering course in English to keep his brain cells alive. He's missing a lot of fun in becoming part of the country.

Edwin Salas is the inspired, imaginative head of the ICT's Pensionado Department. Officially it's Departamento de Jubilados, Instituto Costarricense de Turismo, Apto. 777, San Jose, Costa Rica. Telephone, 23-17-33, Ext. 264. His advice is the best I've heard: "When you're deciding to retire here, think about your attitude toward foreigners at home and then toward Costa Ricans. You'll find the villagers kind and generous as long as we don't feel rejected. Costa Ricans are very sensitive. An approved pensionado is a Costa Rican. Most U.S. citizens are scared by the language barrier. Don't be scared; it is not a barrier. There are so many fields in Costa Rica that the ground is fertile but we need the seed."

Sr. Salas and others give a Newcomers' Seminar the second Tuesday of every month at the Irazú Hotel to which all are invited. If you're thinking of retiring here, come and ask questions and meet others who already have.

Costa Rica needs volunteers from babysitters to engineers and doctors. Sr. Salas took an inventory of much of the country's volunteer needs and would be very glad to point anyone interested toward a spot that could use his or her skills. It's the best way I've heard to get behind the doors and walls and meet interesting people as well as gain a sense of accomplishment. Volunteers have designed roads and helped train local medical helpers. The pensionado office has 18 part-time volunteers who have designed its layout, put its records on computer, and who can translate 7 languages to help any retiree who needs it.

I think retiring here, or perhaps anywhere, is like the fenceposts you'll see along the road. If a dead log is set, it soon rots in the tropics. Costa Ricans plant live poro tree trunks with the bark left on. They grow into trees that work as fenceposts for a lifetime. You can keep living and growing or rot.

If you're thinking of moving here, there are two pieces of advice you'll hear everywhere: come for extended visits, including one of at least 6 months; and don't cut yourself off by handling your assets so that you can't return to your native country temporarily or permanently later if you change your mind.

The paperwork and procedure for becoming a pensionado are no one's joy. Start with ICT's advice in the Pensionado Office and talk to a lawyer recommended by other pensionados who've weathered the process. Be sure any time you deal with immigration that you have all the documentation of birth, bank and pension records they require. There is an effort being made now to simplify the process and to remove taxes recently added by the legislative assembly.

You will be able to bring in $7000 worth of household goods once (including freight costs in that value) and a vehicle every 5 years without paying the usual duties. At this writing there is a new tax on part of that value, but it will probably be removed.

Do be prepared with patience to earn at least part of that pensionado status by outlasting the procedure for getting it.

And then call the Pensionado Office and pitch in to make a contribution here!

Hired help for house and yard costs much less here than elsewhere, but you must get references from past employers for anyone who will be in the house when you aren't there. A good live-in maid is an excellent deterrent to theft. Be prepared to explain exactly how you want anything done, if necessary in sign language at first while the maid teaches you Spanish! Many houses come with maid's quarters built in and you provide food. Costa Rican law provides for at least half a day off per week, holiday

Costa Rican children enjoy trick or treating at Halloween.

and vacation pay, and severance pay for anyone who has worked at least a year for you. With vacation and severance, you pay 14 months pay for a 12 month year. You will also have to make social security contributions.

Your maid can help with or do the marketing and is a real asset when you bargain for produce or simply want to pay tico instead of gringo prices for anything not in major stores. She may be able to recommend seamstresses, haircutters, and neighborhood cab drivers who can be counted on at 5 a.m. when you need to catch an early flight. She can show you how to make tortillas, but you may have to show her how you want eggs fried.

If you want to bring a dog or cat into Costa Rica, you need to write ahead to Jefe del Departamento de Zoonosis, Ministerio de Salud, 1000 San Jose, Costa Rica, C.A. Ask for a form for Importation Permission. There will be a small fee required when you send it back (make a copy first in case it is lost in the mail). Allow time for the validated form to get back to you. You also need a health certificate signed by a local vet and certified by a Costa Rican consul. The health certificate needs to state that the animal is free of internal and external parasites, and in the case of a dog, has had shots for distemper, hepatitis, leptosporosis, and parvovirus, and has a rabies shot at least 30 days old but not more than 3 years old. With all of this done in time, the entry is very smooth at the airport.

When I took my German Shepherd to Costa Rica for 2 months, I went first to her vet at home and got a store of worm pills and flea and tick dip. She caught a mild bout of canine turista probably from drinking ditch water on our morning jogs, but that easily cleared with terramyacin. Note that very short-haired dogs are vulnerable to stinging insects and the screw worm fly which lays its eggs under the skin of livestock, leaving a large abcess with the larva. A medium coat seems to be adequate protection. I wouldn't consider taking any pet on a short trip as it vastly complicates finding housing—and, remember that $1 a pound in excess baggage!

Returning to the U.S. was simple. A Costa Rican vet filled out another health certificate which I took to the Dept. of Zoonosis in the Ministry of Health building behind San Juan de Dios Hospital, Calle 16, Ave. 6/8. It took just a few minutes and a few colones for the revenue stamp (much easier than getting *my* exit visa). All the U.S. authorities required at the border was the rabies certificate.

There are good vets and boarding kennels in the San Jose area. If you'll be living outside the Meseta Central, you may want to make up a pet medical kit. If you will be living on the coast, you might think again before bringing a cold weather breed. There are well-bred dogs available in Costa Rica.

Learning Spanish

You say you had 2 years of Spanish in high school 30 years ago, taught by the football coach because he had to have a few class hours? Costa Ricans appreciate any effort you make to speak their language. It shows that you care about them and their culture, besides making travel easier and allowing you to meet a wider variety of people than if you can only speak to those with English. They will help you with it and tell you words, unless they're too busy practicing their English on you! They also speak a bit more slowly than some Latin Americans which gives you a chance.

If you can, take a class before you leave home. There are now some excellent tape language courses you can practice at home, from quick travelers' phrases needed in restaurants to the level the State Department employees are supposed to know. In between are some for the business traveler. Most of these now stress Latin American Spanish rather than 18th century Castilian. If you call the Spanish teachers at the nearest community college or adult education program, they may have a class, know where there's a Spanish conversation club, or help you find a good native speaker who'd like someone to practice English with in return. Classes in US schools used to stress reading and didn't help you listen and speak very much.

In San Jose there are excellent Spanish schools which teach short and long courses, some of which are very intensive. The Costa Rican-North American Cultural Center in Los Yoses has an excellent library, offers classes and programs at reasonable

102

cost. It's a good place to meet people, both Costa Rican and foreign residents. In Los Yoses, on the main route leaving San Jose to the east. Apto. 1489, 1000 San Jose. Telephone 25-73-44. The *Tico Times* has ads for most schools.

You will be surprised how fast you can pick up some Spanish if you're not shy about trying to use it and make the effort to speak with local people instead of talking mostly to fellow foreigners. Spanish is probably the world's easiest language, and once you learn some, more doors are open in Costa Rica and you're set for travel all over Latin America.

Palm nut plantation. Oil is pressed from these nuts, grown on many acres near Quepos. (ICT)

Investing in Costa Rica

We've mentioned agricultural projects for which you'll see investment advertising—for plantations of established and new crops such as macadamia nuts, jojoba oil, oranges, cardamom

103

(spice), vanilla, and cashew nuts. You'll also see ads for real estate developments, either as raw land or condominiums, built or not yet constructed. There are industrial plants and tourist developments seeking investment capital.

You will have to make your own assessment of the projects and of the honesty and business sense of those promoting them. It's definitely "buyer beware." You're wise to live in Costa Rica for awhile, at least on extended visits, and see the project on the ground as well as look at similar projects before investing. You'll want to have someone honest with excellent Spanish, if yours is not, read any documents before you invest or sign. Many projects are promoted by foreigners rather than Costa Ricans.

Note also that many agricultural projects make heavy use of the pesticides and herbicides exported liberally by US chemical companies to Third World countries where their use isn't banned or controlled as it may be at home. Sometimes the names of products are changed so you can't recognize them (e.g. read the billboards along the road up Irazú) and the instructions and cautions are written in English so the campesinos using them may not dilute or apply as directed.

Real estate in the Meseta Central is controlled and so are building permits much as they are where you come from (check to see if you'll be able to build on the lot). Outside the area, some developers have simply run bulldozers wherever it would make the most lots without regard for the land, slope, or erosion. There are also some excellent projects (look during or just after the rainy season).

In addition to concern for the safety of your investment, it will be up to you and your conscience where you draw the line on chemical use or on real estate developments which raise the price of Costa Rican land beyond the ability of Costa Ricans to buy their own—or send it to the sea more rapidly than nature intended. Some projects are extremely well designed and well managed. The choice is yours.

The Cultural Plaza in downtown San Jose. Below street level are the gold museum, the tourist information center, and galleries for art exhibits.

REGIONS

Meseta Central

The Meseta Central, often called the Central Valley, is the heart of Costa Rica. High enough to be comfortable all year just north of the equator, with never a frost, and little need for either heat or air conditioning, it's an ideal climate for people, most flowers and plants, and for doing whatever you want to almost any day of the year. Here there's a variety of scenery at every turn. Each village has a different character to explore, and the center of it all is bustling San Jose.

San Jose

San Jose is by far the largest city in the country, surrounded by a cluster of communities whose residents commute to work in the city daily. All national capitals should be this size—just big enough to be a city with fine restaurants, night clubs, excellent hotels in all price ranges, and cultural activities of all kinds. From discotheques, movie theaters with films in several languages, to big and little theater groups, sports events, art galleries, museums, shopping for anything, it's all here in a city small enough for you to walk around the central part in a day and to leave in a few minutes by bus or car. You can explore the city for a few days and vary your trip with day tours to nearby towns in the Meseta Central or up the nearby volcanoes as well as to each coast. People watching, night or day, is always entertaining.

When the stone sidewalks get hard, you can sit in one of the many parks for peace even a few feet from the busy streets. Do watch your step on the sidewalks as most are the responsibility for maintenance of the property owners they pass—and the stones and concrete vary accordingly. Some parks are the scene of weekly band concerts or art shows.

Stop by the ICT information desk under the Cultural Plaza at Ave. Central and Calle 5 for information and maps. Pick up the latest issue of the *Tico Times* at the newsstand on the west side of the Plaza, and you'll see what an array of choices you have. Now those addresses we've been using so freely without explanation—San Jose is really very easy to find your way around in, especially on foot when you don't have to worry about one-way streets. Do assume, however, that pedestrians have no rights. That assumption can save your life!

San Jose's streets run north and south, the *calles*. *Avenidas* run east and west. Near the center of town is Avenida Central. North of it all the avenidas are numbered in odd numbers, to the south in even numbers. Actually Avenida 2 (Dos or Segunda) is a bigger boulevard in downtown than Central. On the west end of downtown, west of San Juan de Dios Hospital, Avenida Central is called Paseo Colón and is a wide, tree-lined street ending at Sabana Park. Calle Central runs north and south near the center of town and the streets to the east are numbered in odd numbers, to the west in even numbers. Numbers are usually on the corner buildings rather than on street signs. But there aren't any building numbers, and directions are in meters or varas from a corner. A block is supposed to be 100 varas long, a bit less than a hundred yards. An address might be given as a 3 c 5/7. That means the building faces Avenida 3 on the block between Calles 5 and 7. It may be on either side of the street. It gets more sporting in the suburbs or out of town when everything is in meters.

Besides the sights we've already discussed in San Jose, you might want to look at the small national zoo (entrance on Calle 9, Ave. 11) where there are examples of much of Costa Rica's bird and animal life. The zoo will be moved to a larger site in the western suburb of Santa Ana, but that isn't completed yet. If you're lucky, you might see one of the sloths in the trees landscaping the zoo. A small shop sells T-shirts and other souvenirs to help raise money for the zoo and other parts of the national park system. You can get information about some of the other parks and their wildlife there as well.

The National Liquor Factory, a government enterprise, is on Calle 11 between Ave. 3/7. You can watch liquor made from Costa Rican fruits.

At night it's best to walk in groups if you go through the parks, but the Plaza de la Cultura is a busy spot and worth a stroll any night you're downtown. On a balmy evening, several small bands may be playing, teenagers may be dancing to tape recorders, a student orchestra may be playing at the bottom of the stairs outside the ICT information office, street performers may be juggling—wander by and see what's happening tonight. You can often get tickets to National Theater performances even at the last minute, but it's best to get them earlier if possible.

San Jose is a city to enjoy, and the gateway to all the other things to see and do in Costa Rica.

Where to Stay

San Jose hotels:

Aurola Holiday Inn: Opening in 1985. Convention facilities, casino.

Cariari: Luxury hotel on grounds of Cariari Country Club. Some suites. Rate includes breakfast, full use of country club except golf green fees and horse rental. Tennis, riding school, jumping course, international class golf course. Convention facilities, discotheque, casino.

Herradura: Luxury hotel adjacent to Cariari Country Club, with full use of facilities. TV direct from US by satellite. Church with mass in Spanish & English. Convention facilities for meetings of 10-200 people. Both hotels above are between airport and San Jose.

Playboy: Near Sabana Park at west end of San Jose. Many rooms with view of mountains. Tennis, sauna, large pool in court with bandstand. Convention facilities.

Ambassador: Outer rooms have mountain view over street, inner rooms face landscaped well. 6th floor all suites. Allows pets on approval.

Balmoral: Conversational lounges on each floor. Some interior rooms face center well. Double glass on front cuts noise. Rooms big. Convention facilities, casino, laundry, suites. Downtown.

Gran Hotel Costa Rica: Overlooks Plaza de la Cultura and plaza in front of National Theater. Suites. Inner court and garden with glass elevator. Dining room top floor. Coffee shop on ground floor with terrace is good place for sightseeing break.

Irazú: Biggest hotel in Costa Rica, just outside town on freeway. All rooms have balcony, tub & shower. Lighted tennis courts, beauty shop, sauna, casino, suites. Convention facilities.

Royal Dutch: Cafeteria. Pleasant rooms, well furnished, sitting areas. Suites. Quieter in back rooms.

Torremolinos: Cable TV (English), sitting area even in smallest rooms. Sauna, landscaped courtyard, quiet neighborhood at edge of downtown.

Europa: Only downtown hotel with pool. Some rooms with balcony overlooking pool in inner court. Large rooms, suites.

Town: San Jose

Hotel	Address	Telephone	No. of Rooms	w/Bath	In Town	Courtesy Transp.	Air Cond or Fan	Parking	Restaur't	Bar	Elevator	TV	On Waterfr't	Pool	English Spoken	Noise Level	Cleanli-ness	Price Range
Aurola Holiday Inn	Calle 5, Ave. 5, Apdo. 2028, 1000 San Jose	23-30-66	220	all	x	x	A/C	x	3	3	x	x		x	x	not insp.	not insp.	A
Cariari	Autopista general Cañas, Apdo. 737, 1000 San Jose	39-00-22, Telex: 7509 Cariari	154	all			A/C	x	x	x		x		x	x	exc.	exc.	A
Herradura	Autopista general Cañas, Apdo. 7-1880, 1000 San Jose	33-00-33, Telex: 7512 Herratel	120	all			A/C	x	2	3		x		x	x	exc.	exc.	A
Playboy	Autopista general Cañas, Apdo. 2443, 1000 San Jose	32-81-22, Telex: 2700 LaBoy	140	all	x	x	A/C	x	x	x	x	x			x	exc.	exc.	A
Ambassador	Calle 26/28, Ave. Ctl. Apdo. 10186, 1000 San Jose	21-81-55, Telex: 2315 Ambassador	71	all	x	x	A/C	x	x	x	x	x			x	exc.	exc.	B
Balmoral	Calle 7/9, Ave. Ctl. Apdo. 3344, 1000 San Jose	22-50-22	150	all	x		A/C		x	x	x	x			x	exc.	exc.	B
Gran Costa Rica	Calle 5, Ave. Ctl./2. Apdo. 527, 1000 San Jose	21-40-00, Telex: 2131 Hotel Rica	104	all	x				x	x	x	x			x	exc.	exc.	B
Irazú	Autopista general Cañas, Apdo. 962, 1000 San Jose	32-48-11	350	all		x	A/C	x	x	x	x	x		x	x	exc.	exc.	B

Price ranges for single room: A, over $52; B, $36-52; C, $24-36; D, $13-24; E, $7-13; F, up to $7. Plus 13% tax.

San Jose has many lovely parks, including Parque Morazán.

La Gran Via: Rooms at back very quiet. Front rooms have balcony overlooking street. Cafeteria, coffee shop.

Costa Rica Tennis Club: Very quiet on street off south side Sabana Park (with jogging paths). Rooms pleasant, on 2 floors. Sauna, 8 tennis courts, bowling, basketball, huge pool. Excellent value.

Alameda: Rooms at back quieter. Phone in room. Up to 5 beds for family in some rooms. Neighborhood looks rough after dark.

Amstel: Well-run, with super food. Rooms with air conditioning slightly higher. Rooms facing Calle 7 quietest. Central, good neighborhood. Excellent value. Dutch management.

Bougainvillea: New in 1984. Same management, slightly higher than Amstel. Quiet street. Wheelchair accessible. Bathrooms have tub & shower.

Town San Jose, cont.

Hotel	Address	Telephone	No. of Rooms	w/Bath	In Town	Courtesy Transp.	Air Cond or Fan	Parking	Restaur't	Bar	Elevator	TV	On Waterf't	Pool	English Spoken	Noise Level	Cleanliness	Price Range
Royal Dutch	Calle Ctl., Ave. Ctl. Apdo. 4283 1000 San Jose	22-14-14 Telex: 2925 RDutch	67	all	x		A/C		x	x	x	x			x	good	exc	B
Suites Royal Dutch	Calle 4, Ave. Ctl./2 Apdo. 4.258	33-50-33	27	all	x		some		x	x	x	x			x	good -exc	exc	B
Torremolinos	Calle 40/ Ave. 5 Apdo. 2029	22-52-66 Telex: 2343 Hotomol	73	all	x	x	A/C	x	x	x		x		x	x	quiet	exc	B
Europa	Calle Ctl., Ave. 3/5 Apdo. 72	22-12-22 Telex: 3242 Europa	72	all	x	x	some		x	x	x	x		x	x	exc.	exc	C
La Gran Via	Calle 1/3, Ave. Ctl. Apdo. 1.433	22-77-37	32	all	x		A/C		x	x	x	x			?	exc.	exc.	C
Costa Rica Tennis Club	Sabana sur Apdo. 4.964	32-12-66	26	all	x		A/C	x	x	x	x	x		x	x	exc.	exc.	C
Alameda	Calle 12/14, Ave. Ctl. Apdo. 680	22-60-94	52	all	x		some			x						good	very good	D
Amstel	Calle 7, Ave. 1/3 Apdo. 4192	22-46-22	55	all	x		some		x	x						good	exc.	D
Bougainvillea	in front of Edificio del Monte Apdo. 169 2120 San Jose	33-86-22 Telex: 3300 Bougai	57	all	x		fans	x	x	x		x				exc.	exc.	D

Price ranges for single room: A, over $52; B, $36-52; C, $24-36; D, $13-24; E, $7-13; F, up to $7. Plus 13% tax.

Fortuna: Helpful management. Family hotel. Good neighborhood. Beautiful Chinese restaurant with garden on ground floor. Weekly rates.

Galilea: Rooms quieter at back. Pleasant. 1/2 block from Cartago bus station.

Plaza: Small lounge each floor. Management helpful. Phone in room. Rooms small but adequate. Good value.

President: Price range depends on room size. Phones. Suite. Inside rooms have windows to halls and skylighted wells, so are airy & quiet.

Talamanca: Large pleasant rooms, good beds. Bathrooms needed scrub. Take credit cards.

Bella Vista: Some rooms have windows open to center, planted well—quiet. Not all rooms have windows. Hot water. Two floors.

Boston: Rooms larger than most similar hotels. Back rooms quieter, open to stairwell. Hot water. Good value, and neighborhood.

Cocorí: Back rooms quieter. Beds and bathrooms modern and excellent. Clean soda downstairs. Rough neighborhood but C. is best in it, adjacent to bus to Liberia.

Diplomat: Pleasant, cheerful rooms. Good neighborhood.

Johnson: Sitting area each floor. Phones. Restaurant serves breakfast only.

Pension Costa Rica Inn: Manager very helpful. Good tipico hotel in good neighborhood, feels like Costa Rica. Usually has many North Americans who live in country.

Petit: Very Pleasant with good beds. Manager helpful. Sitting room with some rooms. Cheerful, in good neighborhood.

Town: San Jose, cont.

Hotel	Address	Telephone	No. of Rooms	w/Bath	In Town	Courtesy Transp.	Air Cond or Fan	Parking	Restaur't	Bar	Elevator	TV	On Waterfr't	Pool	English Spoken	Noise Level	Cleanli-ness	Price Range
Fortuna	Calle 2/4, Ave. 6 Apdo. 7.1570	23-53-44	30	30	x				x	x					x	good -exc.	exc.	D
Galilea	Ave. Ctl., Calle 13	33-69-25	23	all	x			x							x	good exc. in back	exc.	D
Plaza	Calle 2/4, Ave. Ctl. Apdo. 2019	22-55-33	40	all showers	x					x	x	x	x			x	good exc.	exc.	C
President	Ave. Ctl., Calle 7/9 Apdo. 2922	22-30-22	47	all	x					x	x	x	x			x	exc.	exc.	D
Talamanca	Calle 8/10, Ave. 2 Apdo. 449 1002 P. Estudiantes	33-50-33	54	all	x					x	x	x				x	good	fair -good	D
Bella Vista	Ave. Ctl., Calle 19/21 Apdo. 3151	23-00-95	17	all	x				x	x	x		x			x	good	exc.	E
Boston	Ave. 8, Calle Ctl./2 Apdo. 5506	21-05-63	25	all	x												very very good good in back	very good	E
Cocori	Calle 16, Ave. 3	33-00-81	26	all	x					x	x	x					good exc.	exc.	E
Diplomat	Calle 6, Ave. Ctl./2 Apdo. 6.606	21-81-33	30	all	x					x	x	x					v. good	good	E
Johnson	Calle 8, Ave. Ctl.	23-76-33	57	all	x					x	x	x				x	good	fair	E

Price ranges for single room: A, over $52; B, $36-52; C, $24-36; D, $13-24; E, $7-13; F, up to $7. Plus 13% tax.

113

Ritz: North American manager. Popular with foreign students, businessmen. Friendly place. Breakfast served. Rooms at back quieter. Lobby with TV, plants. Good value.

Troy's: Small friendly place with North American manager just east of central city. Simple meals served. Lobby with cable TV in English. Good value.

Asia: Helpful Chinese manager. Rooms quieter at back. Small lounge.

Astoria: Hot water and washing machine. Friendly manager. Most rooms don't have windows. Garden courtyard in back, TV in lobby.

Boruca: Small, clean. Some rooms with no windows, partitions to hall open at top (ventilation, but quiet depends on other guests).

Centroamericano: Room windows open to hall with plants. No street noise. Small lobby with TV. Hotel busy with foreign and tico residents.

Musoc: Friendly place, Peace Corps hangout. One of few in this price range with hot water. Rough neighborhood overlooking Coca Cola bus terminal but could get company if going out at night.

Pension Americana: Hot water. Six-bed dormitory and single rooms same price (less than $3). Lobby with TV. Family place used by ticos.

Pension Otoyo: Pleasant owner with limited English has been in business for 30 years. Light and airy with tile hallways, plants, TV in lobby. Tipico basic hotel in good neighborhood. Good value.

Poás: Pleasant, tipico basic hotel with hot water in good neighborhood for less than $3. Clean, inexpensive restaurant. Street level.

Town — San José — cont.

Hotel	Address	Telephone	No. of Rooms	w/Bath	In Town	Courtesy Transp.	Air Cond or Fan	Parking	Restaur't	Bar	Elevator	TV	On Waterfr't.	Pool	English Spoken	Noise Level	Cleanliness	Price Range
Pension Costa Rica Inn	Calle 9, Ave. 1/3 Apdo. 10282	22-52-03	35	all	x										x	good	exc	E
Petit	Calle 24, Ave. Ctl./2 Apdo. 1172 Centro Colon	33-07-66	17	12	x			x	x	x						very good	very exc	E
Ritz	Calle Ctl., Ave. 8/10	21-41-03	16	most	x										x	good -exc.	good exc	E
Troy's	Ave. 2, Calle 19/21	22-67-56	5	3	x				x	x					x	exc.	exc.exc	E
Asia	Calle 11, Ave. Ctl./1	23-38-93	15	1	x										x	good	good good	F
Astoria	Apdo. 7427 Ave. 7, Calle 7/9	21-21-74	22	3	x				x	x						exc.	exc. exc	F
Boruca	Calle 14, Ave. 1/3	23-00-16	24	0	x											fair	very good	F
Centroamericano	Calle 6/8, Ave. 2 Apdo. 3.072	21-33-62	45	all	x				x	x						good	good fair	F
Musoc	Calle 16, Ave. 1/3	22-94-37	49	23	x											fair	very good	F
Pension Americana	Calle 2, Ave. Ctl. Apdo. 4853	21-41-71	32	0	x										x	fair	good	F
Pension Otoyo	Calle Ctl., Ave. 5/7 Apdo. 6226	21-39-25	13	7	x										x	very good	very good	F
Poás	Ave. 7, Calle 3/5	21-78-02	18	0	x											good	exc.	F

Price ranges for single room: A, over $52; B, $36-52; C, $24-36; D, $13-24; E, $7-13; F, up to $7. Plus 13% tax.

The tapir in the San Jose zoo is thoroughly adjusted to people. In the wild, you're lucky to see tracks.

Roma: Hotel upstairs, with hot water for less than $3. Beds soft and ventilation inadequate. Basic hotel in so-so neighborhood.

Apartotels in and near San Jose:

Castilla: Excellent quiet neighborhood off Paseo Colón. 1 and 2 BR apartments with living and dining room, parquet floors, kitchen and laundry room, 4-burner stove. 10% monthly disc. One BR apartments open to well, quiet. Two BR apartments have balcony facing quiet street.

Conquistador: 200 mts. north of Almacen Electra and bus stop, San Pedro bus. Large pool and wading pool, walled garden. Most 2nd floor rooms have mountain view. Cheapest are studio apartment, others have separate living room, all are roomy. Tiled floor, 3- or 4-burner stove. Pets allowed. $4/day. Recommended.

Town: San Jose, cont.

Hotel	Address	Telephone	No. of Rooms	w/Bath	In Town	Courtesy Transp.	Air Cond or Fan	Parking	Restaur't	Bar	Elevator	TV	On Waterfr't	Pool	English Spoken	Noise Level	Cleanli-ness	Price Range
Roma	Paseo Colon/Calle 14	23-21-79	50	3	x			NOT INSPECTED								good	very good	F
Apartotel Pacifica	San Francisco de Dos Rios, Apdo. 3063	22-65-18	6	6	x													B
Apartotel Napoleon	Calle 40, Ave. 5, Apdo. 8-6340	23-32-52	26	all	x			x	x			x		x	x	exc.	exc.	C
Apartotel Ramgo	near Tennis Club, Apdo. 1441	32-38-23 / 32-33-66	16	all	x			x				x				exc.	exc.	C
Apartotel San Jose	Calle 17/19, Ave. 2, Apdo. 5834	22-04-55	12	all	x			x				x				good	exc.	C
Apartotel Castilla	Calle 24, Ave. 2/4, Apdo. 4699	22-21-13 / 21-20-30	15	all	x			x				x				very good	exc.	D
Apartotel El Conquistador	Los Yoses, Apdo. 303, San Pedro Montes de Oca, San Jose	24-24-55 / 24-21-66	29	all (suburb)	x			x	x			x		x	x	exc.	exc.	D
Apartotel Lamm	Calle 15, Ave. 1, Apdo. 2729	21-49-20	20	all	x			x				x			x	good	exc.	D
Apartotel Los Yoses	Carretera San Pedro, Apdo. 1597	25-00-33	23	all (suburb)	x			x						x			fair	exc.	D
Motel Bemo	Sabana Norte		20	all	x				x	x			NOT INSPECTED					C

Price ranges for single room: A, over $52; B, $36-52; C, $24-36; D, $13-24; E, $7-13; F, up to $7. Plus 13% tax.

Lamm: Near legislative assembly. Very helpful owner speaks fluent English. Separate bedroom, kitchen and living room. Some suites with maid's quarters. Daily linen change. Laundry and dry cleaning on premises. 24 hour porter and switchboard service. Can order refr. stocked before arrival. Weekly disc. No. pets. Recommended.

Los Yoses: Some without kitchen facilities. Floor plans vary. Some have BR curtained from living room. 3-burner stove. Safety boxes. Medium-sized pool. Monthly disc.

Napoleon: Coffee shop. Residential neighborhood near Sabana Park (3-4 blocks). Some floors carpet, some tile. Cheap rooms no kitchen. Kitchen units have 2-burner stove. Pets allowed.

Pacifica: Not inspected. Southeast corner of San Jose.

Ramgo: On quiet street across from south side Sabana Park. Supermarket 1 block. Has lawn with courtyard. All apartments have 2 BR, roomy kitchen, laundry room, 4-burner stove, color TV. Small pet OK. Weekly and monthly rates. Embassy personnel use.

San Jose: 1 BR apartments have no table, only dining counter. 2 BR apts. have table. Parquet floors. Living room has day bed. Apts. smaller than some. Weekly, monthly rates.

Motel Bemo: On north side Sabana Park. Not inspected.

The following hotels in San Jose were not inspected. Most are basic to budget hotels. If that's your interest, you may want to look at them. I'd start with the ones that have *both* calles and avenidas in *odd* numbers, for a better neighborhood.

America, Ave. 7, Calle 2/ctl. **Capital,** Calle 4, Ave. 3/5. 15 rooms, restaurant and lounge. Phone 21-84-97. **Central,** Calle 6, Ave. 3. **Concordia,** Calle 24, Ave. ctl/Paseo Colón. This one was closed when I stopped there once. Neighborhood OK. **Lido,** Ave. 3, near Calle 14. **Lincoln,** Calle 6, Ave. 10/12. **Ostuma Inn,** Ave. 9, Calle 9/11. **Pension Acosta,** Ave. ctl., Calle 12/14. I found the entrance too forbidding and didn't get further. **Pension Canada,**

118

Calle 9, Ave. 7/9. **Principe**, Ave. 6, Calle ctl./2. This neighborhood wouldn't be bad. Phone 22-79-83 Apdo. 4450, 1000 San Jose. 48 rooms. **Rialto,** Ave. 5, Calle 2. **Sheraton,** Ave. ctl., Calle 12/14. 56 rooms. **Tala Inn,** Calle 11, Ave. 7/9.

Outlying hotels in the Meseta Central vary from basic hotels you'll find in any town in the country to small super-deluxe quiet places on hills overlooking the valley. These include some of the plushest hotels in Costa Rica.

Los Portales: Six of the most regal suites you can find anywhere in the world. Each has a fireplace, bar, barbecue, 2 balconies, huge bathroom with sunken tub, and 2 queen-sized beds. Several swimming pools with night lights overlooked by candlelit dining room. Tennis courts. On hill above Escazú. Canadian owners.

El Pórtico: 8km. above Heredia in hills. Rebuilt after fire, it has polished burnt brick original dining room floor (beautiful). Hotel is very well done with heavy beams and hardwoods. Large rooms. Helpful management. "We have lots of tranquillity." They have smashing views and lovely nearby walks on slopes of Barva Volcano. Residents are often other Central Americans on weekends. Cater to seminars during week. Excellent value.

Note that in this volcanic belt every hotel in San Jose has withstood an earthquake of 7.1 on the Richter scale. Emergency lights in stairwells and corridors come on in the event of a power outage. During an earthquake guests are advised to brace themselves in an interior doorway or get under substantial furniture but not to head for the street until the quake is over. Earthquakes are rare and major ones rarer still. They happen more often in any coastal California location.

Since the Roman Catholic church is the principal denomination in any Latin country, the Metropolitan Cathedral (Calle ctl, Ave. 2) and other churches are beautiful expressions of faith, and saints' days are important events. Parades you'll see in San Jose consist mainly of school students, appropriately for this peaceful country. Because San Jose is so cosmopolitan, you will find churches or assemblies of most other denominations in or near the city. If you don't find information on services for yours

Town OUTLYING HOTELS - Meseta Central

Hotel	Address	Telephone	No. of Rooms	w/Bath	In Town	Courtesy Transp.	Air Cond or Fan	Parking	Restaur't	Bar	Elevator	TV	On Waterfr't	Pool	English Spoken	Noise Level	Cleanli-ness	Price Range
Los Portales	above Escazú Apdo. 269 Escazú	28-09-44 Telex: 322Portel	6	all			A/C	x	x	x		x		x	x	exc.	exc.	A
El Portico	above Heredia Apdo. 289 Heredia	37-60-22	14	all			fans	x	x	x		?		x	x	exc.	exc.	D
Motel Cypressal	Heredia		UNDER CONSTRUCTION 1984															
Tirol	San Rafael de Heredia Apdo. 7812 1000 San Jose	23-47-38 21-19-06	10	all		x		x	x	x		?			x	exc.	exc.	D
Motel Rio	Orosí Apdo. 7050 Cartago	51-91-91 51-31-56	7	all				x	x	x		?		x	?	exc.	exc.	E
Posada Pegasus	San Antonio de Escazú Apdo. 370 1250 Escazú	28-41-96	5	all		x		x	x	x	NOT INSPECTED			x nearby	x	exc.	exc.	C
de Montana Gestoria Irazu	above Cartago Apdo. 70690 Cartago	25-86-92 21-62-22	11	all				x	x	x	NOT INSPECTED				exc. Including meals	exc.	F - D
Alajuela	Alajuela Apdo. 110 Alajuela	41-12-41	22	all	x				x	x						exc.	exc.	F

Price ranges for single room: A, over $52; B, $36-52; C, $24-36; D, $13-24; E, $7-13; F, up to $7. Plus 12% tax.

Grand staircase in the National Theater. (ICT)

in the *Tico Times*, ask the ICT or call the *Tico Times* office (29-89-52, 22-00-40).

Banking is a government monopoly with regulations designed not only for safety but to control the flow of foreign exchange in a country which badly needs it. The branch bank across from the Amstel Hotel on Ave. 1, Calle 7, is open Saturday mornings. While foreign banks can't offer a full range of domestic banking services here, the quickest way for North Americans to have money sent to them in Costa Rica is to have it wired to the Bank of America, Ave. Central, Calle 1/3.

Central America's only youth hostel is opening as we go to press, sponsored by Otec, the student organization. Students and teachers from abroad should bring identification as to their status (a letter from school administration on letterhead will do, or bring an international student card). Otec's office is on the ground floor of the same building as ICT's main office, Ave. 4,

Calle 5/7. Mail: Apdo. 323, 1002 San Jose. Tel. 33-27-78, 33-37-25. Otec also runs budget tours for students and teachers in and outside Costa Rica. There is no age limit for full-time teachers or college staff. For students, the maximum age is 25.

Any hotel can do laundry or arrange to have it done. Laundromats may not be self-service but do offer same-day laundry. In San Jose there is one on Paseo Colón near Restaurante Bastille (west of downtown). Lavantia Doña Ana, open Monday through Saturday, is on the Autopista a Zapote, 125 mts. east of Plaza Gonzales, near the Ministry of Public Transport in the southeastern part of town. There's another in the Centro Commercial on the north side of the road to San Pedro, a suburban district east of Los Yoses. Take the San Pedro bus on Avenida 2 and ask the driver to let you off at the right place.

Unless you ride taxis all the time, you'll soon learn the bus routes you need though the others may remain a mystery. Downtown the Sabana Cementario bus runs an elliptical route from Sabana South to town on Ave. Central and 2 and back out on Ave. 3. If you're coming into town from western suburbs, you can catch it at any of several stops near Sabana Park for the ride downtown. Going back out, you can get off near the Coca Cola station area and walk the block or two to that spot to catch your bus home. Try to avoid doing this at rush hour or in the dark, especially the first time. From Los Yoses or San Pedro, the San Pedro bus can drop you a block from the Atlantic Railway station where there are lots of cabs or it's an easy walk downtown. The Alajuela buses leave from the Coca Cola area every 10 minutes or so and stop at the airport. Some are minibuses for a slightly higher rate. ICT has a list of station addresses and they can answer questions.

For buses to Puntarenas, Limón, or Guanacaste, it's wise to get your ticket the day before, and get there about 45 minutes early to be sure of a seat. From Limón back to San Jose, you should do the same.

Alajuela
(pop. 43,000)

Alajuela is a delightful town about 20 km. northwest of San Jose, easily reached by bus, and only a few miles south of the

Alajuela's church has huge dome of dark red corrugated sheet metal (how do they make it curve?).

The altar in Alajuela's beautiful church.

airport. Its cathedral is beautiful with hardwoods inside and dark red shining corrugated metal covering its dome. In front is the central park with a bandstand and spreading mango trees. Another park honors Costa Rica's hero, Juan Santamaria, killed in the battle of Rivas. There's also a museum honoring him which often has current art exhibits. The central market is interesting and open even on Sundays when you might be in Alajuela to catch the special bus that departs from the south side of the church on an excursion up Poás Volcano at 8 a.m.

Nearby attractions include Campestre del Sol, a former country club, with swimming pools, gym and dance hall, open Tuesday through Sunday, 8-4. Tel. 42-00-77. There are soccer games in the stadium almost every Sunday. Between Alajuela and Atenas there's a small private zoo and an adjacent bird zoo with small admission fees. The bus to Atenas can drop you off there. The driver won't speak English, so you'll have to plan what you want to say in Spanish and watch for the sign on the right side of the road several miles out from Alajuela, across from a tropical plant farm, "vivero." Bosque Encantado, Enchanted Woods, is an amusement park in La Garita, with animal sculptures, pool and lake. La Garita also has a hydroelectric dam and many nurseries with house plants. It's fun to walk through such places and take photos if you're traveling and can't take them home. If you buy property in Costa Rica, you'll enjoy low-cost, beautiful plants. At La Guacima there are car and motorcycle races on the track every weekend.

Alajuela Hotel is an exceptional value in a tipico hotel 25 mts. south of the central park. The 4 apartments with living room, kitchen, and 4-burner stove rent for about $4/day single but are usually rented by the month by tourists who can afford to rent them even while touring the rest of the country. The rooms are often rented on the same basis, as it's clean and quiet, though not plush. There's an outdoor laundry area and pleasant lobby. Foreign guests could help you with Spanish, but if you don't have to be in San Jose, this is recommended. It's a quick bus ride to the airport for plane or rental car.

North from Alajuela on the old road, or you can go back out on the autopista to another turnoff, are Grecia, Sarchí, and Zarcero. Grecia is the center of pineapple growing and has an inter-

124

Ojo De Agua (Eye of Water) is a spring gushing over 6,000 gallons of water a minute south of Juan Santamaria Airport. It supplies the city of Puntarenas as well as swimming pools at the site.

Children play in the cascade from Ojo De Agua, squealing in the cold water.

esting church entirely covered in dark red painted metal. Sarchí, as I've discussed, has factories making painted oxcarts in traditional designs and painting the designs on other souvenirs. The furniture alone is worth the trip to see. Farther along, Zarcero is famous for boxwood hedges sculptured into animals and other shapes. There are tours to these towns or you could see them all in a day with a car. Some of the Poás tours stop in Sarchí.

South of the airport, opposite Alajuela, is the spring Ojo de Agua (Eye of Water), where over 6000 gallons of water a minute rush out, supplying water to the city of Puntarenas, several other towns, and several big, clean swimming pools and an amusement area. It's such a popular outing spot, that I'd recommend going on weekdays unless your purpose is people watching. In that case go on Sunday and watch Costa Rican families having fun at one of their favorite places. You can get there by bus or car from San Jose (ask ICT for the bus stop and schedule).

Coffee beans drying in sun are turned frequently by rake to speed drying.

Heredia's old church, now a historic shrine, was built in 1797. The bells, rung during holidays, are from Cuzco, Peru.

Heredia
(pop. 30,000)

Heredia, like Alajuela, is a provincial capital and one of Costa Rica's oldest towns. It's the center of coffee growing and there are several *beneficios* nearby where coffee is dried and hulls removed before shipping. It has an old church, now a historic shrine, with bells brought from Cuzco, Peru, in Spanish colonial times. Several very old buildings, including a Spanish-style fort tower, line the central plaza. From Heredia the road goes over the mountain saddle between the volcanoes, Barva and Poás, to the northern plain. A side road winds to a meeting with the road from Alajuela up Poás, providing an alternate way if you're driving a car and want to see more country. In season you can watch coffee picking; drive carefully to avoid the loaded coffee wagons going from finca to beneficio.

127

Basilica in Cartago, devoted to Costa Rica's patroness saint. (ICT)

Cartago
(pop. 28,000)

Cartago, 14 miles east of San Jose, was capital of Costa Rica during colonial times and later until 1823. At the base of Irazú, it has been shaken by earthquakes during every eruption so there are few old buildings. Several roads and the railroad meet here, making it the marketing and social center for a large area. Buses run between San Jose and Cartago every 20 minutes. Public buses run from Cartago up Irazú with stops at villages along the road twice a day. From here you can also take buses to Orosí and Paraiso.

The parish church in central Cartago, La Parroquia, was damaged by several earthquakes and not rebuilt after the one in 1910. Instead it has been converted into a delightful walled park with ponds, shrubs and benches. The street in front of it is being restored in early style cobblestones.

128

The Basilica of Nuestra Señora de Los Angeles (the Patroness Saint of Costa Rica) is a magnificent Byzantine church on the east side of Cartago. Inside is the tiny image of the Black Virgin, and the walls are lined with cases of the gold and silver gifts by pilgrims in thanks for healing miracles attributed to her. Many are in the shape of body parts healed—hands, arms, legs, etc. The church is built over the spring where the image of the Black Virgin was found. Behind it is a shrine where water from the spring flows and where people bring bottles and other containers to take some of the holy water. The saint's day is August 2, Cartago's biggest annual celebration.

Southeast of Cartago, on the road to Paraiso, are the Lankester Gardens, started by Dr. Charles Lankester as an orchid farm. The farm is now run by the University of Costa Rica biology department and is open to the public for a small fee which helps pay maintenance, from 8 a.m. to 3 p.m. daily. The Paraiso bus from Cartago can let you off there, or you can take a bus tour from San Jose. Orchids are in bloom all year there, but at their peak in March.

Inside Cartago church ruined by earthquake in 1910 Costa Ricans enjoy a park with flowering trees and reflecting ponds.

129

Orosi church, built in 1743, oldest active church in Costa Rica.

Orosi Valley

The Orosi Valley is a beautiful area and a fine day trip from San Jose. There are two scenic overlooks built by ICT with fine views of the valley, picnic facilties, play areas for children, and, at the one overlooking Ujarrás, a restaurant. The Reventazón River winds down the valley, dammed at the lower end by Cachí Dam with hydroelectric project and lake. The village of Orosi is nestled at the head of the valley and has the oldest active church in Costa Rica, built in 1743. It has a small museum. Its simplicity says much about the struggling colonial farmers almost forgotten by Spain but keeping their religion.

Orosi has hot springs and several *balnearios*, public baths. The road circles the valley and crosses Cachí Dam. You can visit the power house.

Below the power house is the river gorge rafted recently by some river guides working in Costa Rica. They scouted it several days before their tip, but arrived to find the water much lower.

By phone they located the manager who asked "How much water do you want?" and then released enough for their trip.

On the north side of the lake is another ICT facility with picnic ground, camping area, playing fields, swimming pool, restaurant, and boat launching ramp for fishing on the lake.

The ruins of Ujarrás church, built in 1693 and abandoned in 1833 when the village was flooded and moved to higher ground, are now a historic shrine. Watch plants now growing between the stones on the walls and try to imagine what this place meant to people so far from Spain.

Coffee plants being bred at CATIE.

Turrialba
(pop. 24,000)

Dropping down into Turrialba on either train or bus, you're passing the lower edge of Costa Rica coffee growing. The town

131

is in a scenic basin at the bottom of Turrialba Volcano. From Turrialba or Cartago one can get by bus to the village of Pacay-as, from which horses or 4-wheel drives will reach the top. The bus to Limón stops for 15 minutes at Turrialba for coffee before you have another steep, beautiful climb over a shoulder of Tur-rialba Volcano to drop down to the eastern lowland. From the top of that ridge you can see the Caribbean Sea.

Turrialba is a good excursion by bus or tour from San Jose to visit the Centro Agronomico Tropical de Investigacion y En-señanza (CATIE). CATIE is a 2500-acre agricultural research station devoted to the needs of the small farmer. Governments of many countries including the United States, Canada, Britain and West Germany support research into high producing, disease-resistant strains of coffee, bananas, cacao. Aside from pollution, the small farmer can't afford agricultural chemicals. Other projects include improved strains of plantain, palms, and livestock bred to grow on coarse tropical grass with little or no grain supplement. A tissue culture lab grows thousands of genetic replicas of each desirable plant for virus-free shipment in small containers all over the tropical world. Agricultural school instructors and researchers in tropical agriculture from many countries study here, living in quarters on the grounds. The world's largest

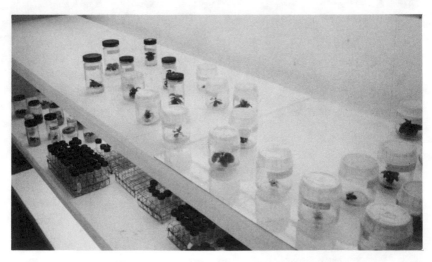

At CATIE, near Turrialba, a modern agricultural research and teaching facility, clones tissue cultures from disease-resistant, high-producing coffee plants for shipment through-out the tropical world.

132

collection of books and papers on tropical agriculture is here, and the card catalog is in English. The station also has a collection of hundreds of palms as well as many other forest species. It's a fascinating place which you can only begin to explore in a day.

If you live in Costa Rica, you may want to talk to them about nursery stock and seed which they sell at very reasonable prices. Dairy products from CATIE are sold in Turrialba, and it is the town's biggest employer.

To tour the station with an English-speaking guide, call 56-64-31 and arrange an appointment. The bus from San Jose will drop you in town (it leaves from the same station as the Cartago buses), and the locals can direct you to the bus that goes by CATIE or you can take a cab from Turrialba. Some tour agencies in San Jose run tours there, and any of them would be glad to set up special tours for interested small groups. At presstime Arnold Erickson from the United States is head of the public relations office there and gives an inspiring tour. If somehow what is learned here can reach the small farmer, there seems more hope of feeding populations without losing or depleting the world's topsoil.

Puerto Limón
(pop. 39,000)

Puerto Limón, capital of the province of Limón, is the only port and the only town larger than a village on Costa Rica's East Coast. Throughout this book we've used Puerto Limón and Limón interchangeably as the people do. After Columbus's landing here in 1502, a permanent Spanish settlement was still delayed for many years by raiding pirates and the lack of obvious wealth. Construction of the train to San Jose and the introduction of Jamaican blacks adapted to the climate led to its growth as Costa Rica's eastern port. Today it's a busy town with modern port facilities being built at Limón and at Moin, its northern suburb.

As it was in Columbus's time, Limón still is hot and humid, and is significant for the tourist mainly as the gateway to attractions north and south and as the end of train or bus from San

133

Jose. The waterfront central park is a pleasant early morning or late afternoon walk with its ornate bandstand and the chance of seeing some of the resident sloths in its trees (look for a motionless blob that looks as if the tide washed it up there, especially on the south side of the park).

Bandstand in park in Puerto Limón. Watch carefully in trees here, especially on the south side of the park, and you may see one of the resident sloths.

Normally sloths only climb down their trees every 7 or 8 days to defecate, but in the dry season these may come down more often for water from park fountains. Local people who find them in the street set them back on their trees, carefully avoiding their 3-inch claws. You may see them peering myopically about or eating a few leaves between naps. For aerobic exercise a sloth scratches his tummy.

There's a small library and roofed open study area for children amid the trees and flowers. Men and boys fish with throw lines from the stone seawall. Several blocks away the central mercado is interesting and has fresh fruit and other supplies you'll want if you're going to stay in villages like Cahuita and Puerto Viejo to the south or in the basic cabinas at Tortuguero.

Like San Jose, Puerto Limón has numbered calles (north-south) and avenidas (east-west, away from shore), except that there are no signs even on buildings and none of the residents seem to have heard of the system! As the shoreline curves deeply into downtown, it's hard to keep count even if you try. If you ask where a hotel is, people will tell you it's so many meters from the park, mercado, or a small radio station. You head in that direction and ask again, or take a cab. Fortunately distances in the downtown area are short and many people are blacks who speak English. There are frequent public buses to Moin which go through Portete.

Columbus Day, October 12, is Limón's big annual festival with street dancing and parades, calypso music, and several days of celebrating. Hotel reservations then are a must.

Most North Americans staying in Limón will require at least a fan keeping air moving to be able to sleep. There are budget and basic hotels in Limón, reviewed below. However, if you can afford more and don't have to catch a 5:30 a.m. bus, it's worth going to one of those at Portete, several miles north. At Moin, the ICT is building a facility including swimming pool, picnic and camping area. Playa Bonita at Portete is Limón's swimming beach.

Where to Stay

Puerto Limón:

Acón: Dining room and food are excellent. Hotel is one of the best in town, but noisy on weekends when discotheque on second floor swings.

Miami: Rooms at back quieter. Soda restaurant serves tipico and Chinese food. Recommended.

Park: Rooms facing sea have fresh air, view and quiet. They fill early in day. Rooms facing street are on block with traffic, 2 cantinas and a firehouse, and without air conditioning, you'll want an open window. Rooms dirty. Dining room recommended. Located 2 blocks from park.

135

Tete: Rooms at back quieter. New bathrooms. Across from mercado. Hotel is on second floor ringed by marble tiled balcony with plants & seats. Helpful manager speaks English.

International: On quiet street. Cold water only, but best choice in downtown for cool, clean, and quiet. Chinese restaurant.

Lincoln: Next door to Internacional on same quiet street. Some rooms have no windows and only 5 have air conditioning, but at $2.50 it's a good value in basic hotel.

Gran Hotel Los Angeles: Across from mercado. Rooms with air conditioning slightly higher. Hot water. Manager helpful. All rooms full; could not inspect.

Ng: Appears clean, basic. Smiling manager refused to show rooms.

Paraiso: Basic, clean. Partitions don't reach ceiling so air moves but quiet depends on guests.

Not inspected: **Caribe,** 58-01-38, 13 rooms. Having found clean if basic rooms for as little as 80 colones near the market and in the next few blocks north, I avoided the rough neighborhood with basic hotels and cantinas near the railroad station.

Portete:

Matama: Deluxe, comfortable concrete cabinas for 6 on landscaped grounds across highway from sea. (2 BR plus loft each) Attractive dining room and lounge. Aviary and tapir on grounds.

Cabinas Cocori: Comfortable but not deluxe cabinas for 4 on water across from Matama, on a point beside small rocky cove, with swimming. Price is per cabina, under $25 for 4, but no single rate.

Las Olas: Deluxe hotel built over beach rocks with covered open air dining overlooking surf and swimming pool. Wheelchair ramp from parking area, sauna (in Limón!), casino. Corner suites with sea view in 2 directions, balcony and sitting room.

Town Puerto Limon – EASTERN REGION

Hotel	Address	Telephone	No. of Rooms	w/Bath	In Town	Courtesy Transp.	Air Cond or Fan	Parking	Restaur't	Bar	Elevator	TV	On Waterfr't	Pool	English Spoken	Noise Level	Cleanli- ness	Price Range
Acon	Calle 3, Ave. 2 Apdo. 528 Puerto Limon	58-10-10	39	all	x		A/C	H	x	x					x	good good	good good	E
Miami	Calle 4/5, Ave. 2 Apdo. 266	58-04-90	30	all	x		A/C	x	x	x						good	very good	E
Park	Ave. 3, Calle 1/2 Apdo. 35 Puerto Limon	58-04-76	25	all	x				x	x			x			good /poor	poor	E
Tete	Apdo. 401 Puerto Limon	58-00-51 58-11-22	14	all	x		bot			x					x	very good /fair	very exc.	E
Internacional	Ave. 5, Calle 2/3 Apdo. 288	58-04-34	20	all	x		A/C		x	x						exc.very good	exc.very good	F
Lincoln	Ave. 5, Calle 2/3 Apdo. 888	58-00-74	15	all	x		A/C			x						exc.very good	very good	F
Los Angeles	Puerto Limon	58-20-68	28	all	x	NOT INSPECTED	A.C		x		NOT INSPECTED					fair exc.	fair exc.	F
Ng	Ave. 5, Calle 3		8															F
Paraiso	Calle 3 or 4, Ave. 4/5	58-06-84	25	shared	x						NOT INSPECTED					varies good	good	F
Caribe	Calle 1, Ave. 2	58-01-38	13						x									F

Price ranges for single room: A, over $52; B, $36-52; C, $24-36; D, $13-24; E, $7-13; F, up to $7. Plus 13% tax.

Organized tours to Cahuita, Tortuguero and Isla Uvita. Excellent value.

There's no bus station, but there are several main bus stops with ticket windows for buses to San Jose and south through Cahuita and Puerto Viejo to Bribri and Sixaola on the Panamanian border, "la frontera." You should buy bus tickets the day before to be sure of getting on and then get there early to get a seat.

SANSA has daily flights between Limón and San Jose, landing at the airport along the road south of town. There's an office downtown in Limón as well as in San Jose.

Taxis wait along the west side of the mercado, even at 5 a.m. when you want to go to Moin to catch a boat. Sometimes you can arrange a reasonable price for a day tour or drop-off at Cahuita or Puerto Viejo for a small group at the time you want to go.

South of Limón there are beaches all along the coast, some with excellent swimming like Cahuita and Puerto Viejo. To the north there are sharks and muddy water from the rivers emptying into the sea. While some people swim at Tortuguero, it can be risky. The sharks follow channels back into fresh water and some go all the way up the San Juan River to Lake Nicaragua. Scientists only recently learned that these sharks move freely back and forth between fresh and salt water.

North From Puerto Limón

Having already described the *canales* as an unforgettable experience for any nature-lover, I won't go into detail here. At presstime the ICT is studying how to make the area more accessible without impact to the natural scene. Presently accommodations range from basic cabinas to deluxe fishing lodges, with nothing in between. Most fishermen using the lodges book weekly package plans before leaving the US or Europe and then fly into the lodge by air taxi. For the very low budget traveler with more time, one could use basic rooms at Tortuguero or Barra Colorado and hire a villager with skiff. Wildlife viewing would then depend on the knowledge of the person you picked.

Town: Portete – EASTERN REGION

Hotel	Address	Telephone	No. of Rooms	w/Bath	In Town	Courtesy Transp.	Air Cond or Fan	Parking	Restaur't	Bar	Elevator	TV	On Waterfr't	Pool	English Spoken	Noise Level	Cleanliness	Price Range
Matama	Plaza Bonita, on road to Portete Apdo. 686 Puerto Limon	58-11-23	8 all cabins	all			A/C	x	x	x				x	x	exc.	exc.	C
Cabinas Cocori	Portete	58-29-30	4 all cabins	all				x	x				x			exc.	exc.	D
Las Olas	Carretera Portete Apdo.301 Puerto Limon	58-14-14	49 all	all			A/C	x	x	x			x	x	x	exc.	very good	D
Parismina																		
Parismina Tarpon Ranch	Parismina	35-77-66 35-94-43	10 all	all					x				x		x	exc.	very good	A
Tortuguero																		
Tortuga Lodge	Tortuguero Apdo. 812,Centro Colon San Jose	71-85-85 35-77-66							x	x			x			exc.	exc.	C
Cabinas Sabina	Barra Del Tortuguera	71-80-99	31		x				x				x			exc.	exc.	F

Price ranges for single room: A, over $52; B, $36-52; C, $24-36; D, $13-24; E, $7-13; F, up to $7. Plus 13% tax.

At Moin, ICT is developing a recreation area with pool, camping, and boat dock for La Samay, the government boat which
cruises as far as Tortuguero. The **Rio Colorado Lodge** runs tours
the full length of the main canal from Moin to Barra and its
lodge there. **Costa Rica Expeditions** and **Swiss Travel** run special
nature tours up the quiet back channels from Tortuguero with
biologists. Shy species such as the manatee are more likely there.
Nature tours generally have to be booked well ahead. Other tour
agents are planning tours in the area.

Where To Stay (south to north)

Parismina Tarpon Lodge: Open Jan.–June for tarpon, Aug.–
Oct. for snook. Fly into local strip, or ride boat short distance
from Moin.

Tortuga Lodge: Deluxe lodge across channel from village,
serves fishermen and nature tours. Open Jan.–June and mid–
Aug. through Oct. Fishing is for tarpon, shark and bass in
spring; snook, shark, and bass in fall. Fall opening during turtle
egg-laying.

Cabinas Sabina: In village of Tortuguero near boat landing.
Basic rooms upstairs slightly higher but have smashing view of
beach and catch breeze. There are other basic rooms not inspect-

Tortuga Lodge at Tortuguero, one of several tarpon and snook fishing lodges on the
northeast coast.

140

Sabina's Cabinas at Tortuguero.

ed, also in village. Small restaurant and pulpería. All adjacent to beach.

Rio Colorado Lodge: Only lodge in area open all year for tours as well as fishing. Can add days to 2 day tours or join tour in Limón if you want to ride train from San Jose. Excellent food, friendly place and staff. Office in Playboy Hotel, San Jose.

Casa Mar: Deluxe fishing lodge, open during fishing seasons. Package fishing trips include almost everything. Not inspected.

Isla de Pesca: Deluxe fishing lodge open mid-Jan.–May 31; Aug.–Oct. 31. Duplex cabins. Tackle shop with sales, rentals. Rates negotiable if group can be coordinated with flight required by another group going or coming. Same management owns fishing camp on West Coast, **Bahia Pez Vela.** Can combine trip with fishing on both coasts if book well ahead.

Rates at all lodges include meals. Fishing tours include boats, guides, equipment, and flight to camp as indicated in package. Some serve liquor extra and with some it's bring your own.

Town Barra Colorado

Hotel	Address	Telephone	No. of Rooms	w/Bath	In Town	Courtesy Transp.	Air Cond or Fan	Parking	Restaur't	Bar	Elevator	TV	On Waterfr't	Pool	English Spoken	Noise Level	Cleanli-ness	Price Range
Rio Colorado Lodge	Barra Del Colorado Apdo. 5094, San Jose	32-40-63 32-86-10	12	all			fan		x	x			x		x	exc.	exc.	B
Casa Mar	Barra Del Colorado Apdo. 176, M. de Oca San Pedro Box 7000-F Redondo Beach, CA 90277	41-28-20 26-51-01 213-540-6293	12	all					x	x			x		x	exc.	exc.	A
Isla de Pesca	Barra Del Colorado Book through: Henry Norton or Mel Schneider 150 E. Ontario Street Chicago, IL 60611	32-82-19 32-22-79	12	all		x			x				x		x	exc.	exc.	A

Price ranges for single room: A, over $52; B, $36-52; C, $24-36; D, $13-24; E, $7-13; F,

Guides are tipped and hotel staff is too if a service charge isn't added.

Barra Colorado is divided by the Rio Colorado with separate villages, Nord and Sud. The airstrip and a basic hotel, not inspected, are at Barra Sud. At Barra Nord there are basic cabinas, also not inspected. High tides and rains can leave both villages soggy and they aren't well lit at night. If you're using basic accommodations, try to avoid a night arrival. The beach at Barra Sud is a steep, wild place not for swimming, but an inspiring walk with driftwood and surf. Sunsets here are some of the world's finest.

South From Puerto Limón

The coastal villages of Cahuita and Puerto Viejo are relaxed places in the Caribbean style of 50 years ago, except for the juke boxes in the cantinas. Accommodations range from budget to basic though clean. You can relax, swim, walk roads and paths to see birds, flowers, monkeys and butterflies, and meet nice people (some of whom are quoted in Paula Palmer's book, *What Happen*). Absorbing the feeling of these villages and understanding what it's like to live here takes time. After 4 days in Cahuita I began to feel in pace and not to feel a reason to hurry, or any "must-dos."

Living is cheap—you'll have to drink a lot to spend more than $7 to $10 a day, and you can get by on less. If you want deluxe hotel rooms, you could stay at Portete and make a day trip south.

Cahuita is larger and more urban, if you can say that about either, than Puerto Viejo. The national park with coral reef adjoins it on the south. Nearby are the hotel and cantinas, and a pulpería, small store with a few groceries and occasional fresh bread. The cabinas are at the end of the point Cahuita is built on and down main street, left at the town power house and another quarter mile on toward the black sand beach. Either area is quiet, lit by fireflies at night.

Puerto Viejo's pace is even slower and more relaxed. It's built around a small bay with calm water for swimming right in front

Puerto Viejo resident stands beside dugout canoe parked on main street. Swimming is excellent here.

Waterfront at Puerto Viejo.

of town. Sanford's, an open-air restaurant overlooking the bay, is well-known for its seafood. In both villages you'll find helpful, genial blacks who speak English, Peace Corps volunteers promoting cooperatives and fish farming, and young, former US residents taking a temporary or permanent break from the hurry back home.

Where To Stay

Cahuita:

Vaz Cabinas: Modern concrete cabinas just being completed early 1984, across from Cahuita Hotel. Owner in Saloon Vaz. Looked comfortable.

Cabinas Jenny: Basic rooms on Cahuita Point, outdoor cooking area. Canadian owned. Friendly place.

Hotel Cahuita: Rooms above and behind small dining room with TV. Food good. Cabinas in back yard probably quieter. Rooms occupied, manager refused to show.

Grant's Cabinas: Separate rooms in cabins, shared bath. One cabina for 2 with shower. Across road from black sand beach. Owner Letty Grant delightful and helpful.

El Atlantida: 2 cabinas with fan, twin beds, on lawn adjacent to soccer field. Canadian owned.

Surfside Cabinas: Modern building on Cahuita Point divided into 2 cabinas for 2-4 people. Excellent value. Mr. and Mrs. David Buchanan are pleasant, interesting mainstays of village.

Puerto Viejo:

Has public phone which may take messages. Unless equipped for camping, be sure you have reservations, especially on weekends.

Apartamentos Antigua Bahio: The only modern, better than basic rooms in town, new in 1983. Pleasant, large rooms, good beds. Rates for 4 and 8 nights.

145

Town: Cahuita - EASTERN REGION

Hotel	Address	Telephone	No. of Rooms	w/Bath	In Town	Courtesy Transp.	Air Cond or Fan	Parking	Restaur't	Bar	Elevator	TV	On Waterfr't	Pool	English Spoken	Noise Level	Cleanliness	Price Range
El Atlantica	Cahuita, Limon	none	2	all	X		fan	X								exc.	exc.	E
Vaz Cabinas	Cahuita, Limon	58-15-15, ext. 218	4	all	X			X							X	good	exc.	E
Cabinas Jenny	Cahuita, Limon		5	shared	X			X					X		X	exc.	very good	F
Cahuita	Cahuita, Limon	58-15-15 ext. 201	20+ 10 cabins		X				X	NOT INSPECTED					X	good	good	F
Grant's Cabinas	Cahuita Apdo. 64, Puerto Limon	58-15-15 ext. 206	6	1	X				X				X		X	exc.	exc.	F
Surfside Cabinas	Cahuita Apdo. 260, Puerto Limon	58-15-15 ext. 202 246	2	all	X			X					X		X	exc.	exc.	F
Apartamentos Antigua Bohio	Puerto Viejo, Limon	58-08-54	2	all	X			X	X				X		X	exc.	exc.	D
Cabinas Manuel Leon	Puerto Viejo, Limon	58-08-54	5	all	X			X	X							good	exc.	F
Maiti	Puerto Viejo, Limon	58-08-54	18		X			X	X	X					X	very good	exc.	F
Maritza	Puerto Viejo, Limon	58-08-54	12		X			X	X				X		X	fair	good	F

Price ranges for single room: A, over $52; B, $36-52; C, $24-36; D, $13-24; E, $7-13; F, up to $7. Plus 13% tax.

146

Grant's Cabinas, clean, with shower and toilet at porch end, offer a chance to try the local lifestyle a few yards from the black sand beach at Cahuita.

Cabinas Manuel Leon: basic rooms in long building. End units have windows on 2 sides, ones in between don't. Rates per unit for 1-3.

Maiti: Rooms basic but screened. Downstairs cheapest, but upstairs light, airy. Manager helpful.

Maritza: Basic rooms on second floor. Music in cantina below supposed to be off at 9 p.m.

West and Southwest

Puntarenas
(pop. 34,700)

Like Limón on the Caribbean coast, Puntarenas is a major port and perhaps more important to the tourist as a gateway to the Gulf of Nicoya and the Nicoya Peninsula than as a long-term destination. Buses and the electric train from San Jose can get you there in a few hours. Puntarenas fills a long narrow sandspit out into the gulf, only a block or two wide at the narrowest. To the south is the open end of the gulf with mild surf hitting the beach. To the north is a lagoon with mangrove swamps, very important to wildlife and fisheries.

If you look quickly as you pass mangroves (one of few trees that grow with roots in salt water) on the right as you start out on the spit, you'll see storks, roseate spoonbills, and other waterfowl feeding in shallow water a few feet from the busy highway. Farther along in the lagoon is Costa Rica's Yacht Club and marina followed by the commercial fishing fleet and the ferry dock. Shrimp fishing is very important here and you may wonder why shrimp is the most expensive item on most menus—it's an export and the price is high to discourage local consumption. The Calypso, a yacht used for very popular day tours in the Gulf of Nicoya, leaves from the yacht harbor. The car ferry leaves twice daily, at 7:30 a.m. and at 4 p.m. for the Nicoya Peninsula. It was built in Denmark and has a stormproof lounge, but you can sit out on deck to enjoy the view. You can also ride a boat to San Lucas Island, a prison colony, where the prisoners sell crafts.

The center of town has several pleasant restaurants with good food and a lovely old church. Like Limón, Puntarenas is hot and humid. I think any person from a temperate climate will need a fan or air conditioning that really makes the air move if you take a room not on the waterfront. Accordingly I didn't inspect the basic hotels in the center of town used by locals. Ask for a demonstration of the fans or air conditioning if you need them.

Along the ocean side of downtown Puntarenas is the Paseo de los Turistas, a tree-lined street and promenade adjoining the beach. There are many soda stands and several hotels. At its far end there's a swimming pool that has been dry the 2 years I've been there. The beach and water here aren't as clean as in other places, though many people swim. Don't leave anything lying unwatched. Several hotels face this beach and some have very clean pools. You definitely need reservations, especially on weekends.

The east or near end of the peninsula if you're coming from San Jose is the Cocal district. There are several deluxe hotels facing the lagoon and perhaps a dozen sets of cabinas facing the ocean, ranging from basic to deluxe. South of the spit is the new ICT recreation area with a camping area at Doña Ana beach, and farther south is the new modern port at Caldera where cruise ships now dock to give their passengers a day tour in Costa Rica as far as San Jose.

Shoreline promenade at Puntarenas. (ICT)

Where To Stay

Note that most hotels on Costa Rica's west coast have high and low season rates, though their definition of the season varies. Most often it's from early December through March. Discounts may be 10-30% in low season. You can get excellent values in November. At presstime the ICT is working to get a general reduction in beach hotel prices in return for tax concessions on imported goods used by the hotels. This could be as much as 40%.

Porto Bello: (Cocal) Deluxe hotel well landscaped, overlooking the lagoon. Best in Puntarenas. Excellent food. Has live music on weekends and can arrange boats and fishing. Same management now has adjacent Colonial Hotel under renovation in early 1984. Whole operation may be combined. Helpful manager.

Costa Rica Yacht Club: (Cocal) Overlooks marina on lagoon; ocean beach across road. Desk staff doesn't speak English. Is possibly closed on Wednesdays.

Tioga: Best hotel downtown. Reservations a must. Price includes American breakfast, the only meal served. Less expensive rooms have cold water only—but that isn't very cold in Puntarenas! Check-out is late, 2 p.m., which may mean you can't get into rooms early in afternoon if coming from San Jose. Don't leave anything visible in car if you park on street! Pool beautiful. Some rooms have ocean view.

Cayuga: On cross street rather than facing waterfront. Many rooms have no windows. Air conditioning units completely ineffective but large and noisy. Hotel not recommended though restaurant is very good.

Los Hamacas: Rooms less expensive without air conditioning, but well lined up with ocean breeze on 2nd floor. Dance floor and bar on 3rd floor are noisy, but hotel otherwise good.

Cabinas Los Joron: Pleasant, roomy cabinas with 2 single and 1 double bed, refrigerator and sink. Clean thatched open restaurant overlooking waterfront. Air conditioning works.

Villas Palmas del Mar: (Cocal) Cabinas (for 5-9 people) surrounding lawn on waterfront, beside highway. Not inspected, but look excellent.

Cabinas San Isidro: (Cocal) Not inspected, but look very good.

Cabinas Chacarita: (Cocal) Inspected because it's nearest the good birdwatching noted earlier, across from the cemetery. Clean, roomy, basic cabinas with ocean breeze, shaded court, stove, and sink. There are other cabinas in the same neighborhood, for perhaps a mile along shore. The following hotel is in

Town Puntarenas – SOUTHWEST REGION

Hotel	Address	Telephone	No. of Rooms	w/Bath	In Town	Courtesy Transp.	Air Cond or Fan	Parking	Restaur't	Bar	Elevator	TV	On Waterfr't.	Pool	English Spoken	Noise Level	Cleanliness	Price Range
Porto Bello (includes Colonial)	Apdo. 108, Puntarenas	61-13-22 61-21-22	34 55	all	x E. end	E. end	A/C	x	x	x			x	x	x	exc.	exc.	B
Costa Rica Yacht Club	Apdo. 1000 Puntarenas	61-07-84 22-38-18	28	all	x E. end	E. end	A/C	x	x	x			x	✓	x	exc.	exc.	D
Tioga	Paseo de Los Turistas Puntarenas	61-02-71	46	all	x		A/C		x	x				x		exc.	exc.	D
Cayuga	Calle 4, Ave. Ctl./1	61-03-44	31	all	x		?		x	x						fair	fair	E
Los Hamacas	Paseo de Los Turistas Puntarenas	61-03-98	24	all	x		A/C (8)	x	x	2			x			good	exc.	E
Cabinas Los Joron	Barrio El Carmen Paseo de Los Turistas	61-04-67	5	all	x		A/C	x	x	x			x	x	x	very good	exc.	E
Villas Palmas del Mar	Cocal District, Puntarenas	61-04-55	11	all	x			x	NOT INSPECTED	x			x			exc.		D
Cabinas San Isidra	Cocal District, Puntarenas	21-12-25 53-00-31	58	NOT	x	NOT INSPECTED	NOT INSPECTED		x				x			very good	very good	E
Cabinas Chacarita	Chacarita, Puntarenas		6	all	x			x								very good	very good	F
Esparza																		
Castanuelas	Esparza	63-51-05	12	all	x		A/C or Fans	x	x							very / exc. good	very / exc. good	E

Price ranges for single room: A, over $52; B, $36-52; C, $24-36; D, $13-24; E, $7-13; F, up to $7. Plus 13% tax.

Jaco Beach is a few hours' drive from San Jose.

Esparza, several miles before you get to Puntarenas, near the junction of the Inter-American Highway and the road to Puntarenas, on the south side of the latter.

Esparza:

Castañuelas: Altitude a bit higher and cooler than Puntarenas, an option if hotels below are full. Large rooms with table, twin beds, trees set back from highway. Price varies whether room has fan or a.c., both effective. Coffee shops nearby. Good value.

Gulf of Nicoya:

Isla Jesusita: On an island in the gulf, reached by public launch or the hotel's own boat. Lodge and cottages, hammocks in shade. Can arrange fishing. Package tours include transportation from San Jose. Not inspected. US toll-free phone: 800-327-9408.

Swimming pool at Jaco Beach Hotel.

Each village in Costa Rica has at least basic hotels used by the locals. South of Puntarenas more tourist accommodations are being built, on Isla Herradura between Puntarenas and Jaco Beach and on the shoreline in the same area. Some aren't well advertised at presstime, but as the road improves and tourism grows, ask ICT what your choices are as it's relatively near San Jose. The best road now is a scenic two-lane road that takes off near Esparza to Orotina and back down to the coast at Jaco Beach.

Jaco Beach

This excellent long beach is easily reached from San Jose and can be crowded on weekends and holidays, as the bus goes there and it's only a 3-hour drive from San Jose via Atenas, San Mateo and Orotina on a scenic hilly paved road.

Where To Stay

Jaco Beach Hotel: Deluxe hotel under same ownership as Irazú in San Jose with a courtesy bus from San Jose. Grounds beau-

153

tifully landscaped adjoining beach. Big, clean pool has island in middle. Large rooms with tub and shower, marble floors and sinks from Guatemala and El Salvador. Newly redecorated wing has elevator, individual balconies facing pool. Suites have refrigerator, sitting room. Good food.

Cocal: Very pleasant, small hotel on beach south of town. Eight rooms face beach with outside decks. Deluxe dining room. Recently acquired from Amstel Hotel in San Jose.

Cabinas Las Palmas: Large clean rooms with 1 double bed & 1 single. Lawn and landscaping with barbecue, a block from beach. Many North Americans stay here. Less than $12/cabina for 1 or 2. Exellent value.

Cabinas Antonio: Lawn, landscaping, pleasant rooms. No fans, but needs them. Otherwise good.

Cabinas Heredia: Freshly painted. Bunk beds. Rooms screened on side facing landscaped yard. Some have no opening at back so no breeze through. Need fans, good otherwise.

At the south end of town there's a private campground just behind the beach with showers, picnic tables and palms. It's a nice area but could have used a clean-up when I saw it.

Esterillos

A new gravel road, soon to be paved, runs down the coast to Quepos and on to Punta Dominical, where it meets a road to San Isidro General and the Inter-American Highway. Esterillos is a seven-mile-long beach with virtually no one on it though it's less than a mile from the main highway. You'll see signs to the west and east ends. Be careful of rips as it's open with surf. Turtles still hatch on beach.

El Delfin: Best designed beach hotel building I've seen. Each room with balcony catching every breeze. Helpful manager. Secluded, beautiful spot. Range C during off season, including November.

Town / Hotel	Address	Telephone	No. of Rooms	w/Bath	In Town	Courtesy Transp.	Air Cond or Fan	Parking	Restaur't	Bar	Elevator	TV	On Waterfr't	Pool	English Spoken	Noise Level	Cleanliness	Price Range
Gulf of Nicoya – WESTERN REGION																		
Isla Jesusita	Apdo. 84 Puntarenas	61-02-63 33-66-64 In U.S.: 1-800-327-9408	?			x	NOT INSPECTED		x						x	exc.		?
Jaco Beach – SOUTHWEST REGION																		
Jaco Beach	Apdo. 962 San Jose	32-48-11 Telex: 2307HotIrazu	150	all	x	x	A/C	x	x	x	x		x	x	x	exc.	exc.	B/A
Cocal	Playa Jaco, Puntarenas c/o Amstel Hotel Apdo. 4192 San Jose	22-46-22	11	all	x	x	fans	x	x	x			x	x	x	exc.	exc.	D
Cabinas Las Palmas	Jaco Beach		11	all	x			x								exc.	exc.	E
Cabinas Antonio	Jaco Beach		11	all	x		fans	x	x							exc.	exc.	F
Cabinas Heredia	Playa Jaco, Puntarenas		12	all	x			x	x							exc.	exc.	F
Esterillos Este																		
El Delfin	Playa Esterillos Este Apdo. 2260 San Jose	71-16-40	15	all			fans	x	x	x			x	x	x	exc	exc	B
Cabinas Los Angeles	Esterillos Este	22-85-03	4				NOT INSPECTED									exc	exc	C

Price ranges for single room: A, over $52; B, $36-52; C, $24-36; D, $13-24; E, $7-13; F, up to $7. Plus 13% tax.

Cabinas Los Angeles: Did not inspect. From back road parallel to beach, looked fairly basic for Range C.

The road continues south through palm nut plantations and several villages, including Parrita, which has a beach and some basic accommodations. Note that beaches near river mouths, as this is, have some mud in the sea.

Fine Brahma bull at pasture.

Quepos

Quepos was a banana port, but now is a marketing center and gateway to Manuel Antonio resorts and beaches. Daily buses and flights from San Jose reach Quepos while shuttle buses and taxis run regularly the few miles on to Manuel Antonio. Quepos has a beach used mostly by locals, a dock area. Basic accommodations, cantinas, and groceries those cooking for themselves at Manuel Antonio need. A mangrove area at the north end of town has good birdwatching morning and night.

Viña del Mar: Hotel on right side entering Quepos from north seems the only better-than-basic place in town. Faces lagoon with another across road. Rooms for 1-5 people, light, airy, with hardwood, but not deluxe.

Manuel Antonio

The 3 beaches, separated by headlands, at Manuel Antonio are as beautiful as any in the world (see our cover). You can drive to the first beach, a long open one with some rip currents that need respect. You wade a creek and walk to the second and third beaches within Manuel Antonio National Pak. These are more sheltered and much safer swimming. Camping is allowed. Some accommodations are adjacent to first beach and others are on the hills above. You should have reservations during holidays when many people from San Jose come. The **Velo Bar**, on a hill above first beach, serves excellent, reasonably priced food. Their seafood dinners are as fine as any in San Jose at a fraction of the cost.

Especially during holidays, you should be concerned about the safety of your valuables while you swim or leave camp, etc. The park entrance station will sometimes keep a day pack for you.

Where to Stay

Mariposa: On ridge above beach with smashing views from every room including the bathrooms. Luxurious, exclusive. Price includes breakfast and dinner. Adult guests only. North American owned. Possibly the finest beach hotel in Costa Rica.

Note that in this area are several other sets of cabinas along the highway, several hundred feet above the north end of first beach. All look OK from the road, but most weren't inspected for this book.

Apartotel Karahe: Cabinas on hill above highway (path down to beach) have daily maid service, cooking facilities, hammock in private area with super view. Rate is per cabina whether 1 or 2 people. Weekly, monthly rates especially in off season. Manager helpful, fluent English. Recommended.

Cabinas Manuel Antonio: Rooms with bunk beds, single story with sitting area in front on beach. Very good value for 4-5 peo-

Town: Quepos – SOUTHWEST REGION

Hotel	Address	Telephone	No. of Rooms	w/Bath	In Town	Courtesy Transp.	Air Cond or Fan	Parking	Restaur't	Bar	Elevator	TV	On Waterf't	Pool	English Spoken	Noise Level	Cleanli-ness	Price Range
Viña del Mar	Apdo. 5527 San Jose	77-00-77	20	all	x		fans	x	x	x			x			very good	exc.	D
Manuel Antonio																		
Mariposa	Manuel Antonio	77-03-55 800-223-6510	10	all			fans	x	x	x					x	exc.	exc.	A
Apartotel Karahe	Apdo. 4, Quepos / Apdo. 100 Quepos	77-01-70	10	all			fans	x						x	x	exc.	exc.	C
Cabinas Manuel Antonio	Manuel Antonio	77-02-12	18	all												exc.	exc.	D
Manuel Antonio	Manuel Antonio, Puntarenas	77-02-90	6	all			fans	x	x	x			x			exc.	exc.	E
Cabinas Ramirez	Manuel Antonio	77-03-03	17	all	x		some fans	x	x	x			x			exc.	exc.	F
Bungalows	Manuel Antonio		6				fans	x	x				x			good	fair	F
Golfito																		
Cabinas Playa Tortuga	Golfito, Puntarenas	75-00-62	5	all			fans						x			exc.	exc.	E
Cabinas Delfina	Golfito	75-00-43	21	7	x		fans	x		x			x			very good	very good	F
El Puente	Golfito	75-00-34	15	all	x		A/C		x						x	very good	very good	F/E
Golfito	Pueblo Civil Golfito	75-00-47	14	all	x		fans	x		x			x		x	exc.	very good	F
Gran Hotel Miramar	Apdo. 21, Golfito	75-01-43	35	18	x		fans	x	x	x			x		x	exc.	exc.	F/E

Price ranges for single room: A, over $52; B, $36-52; C, $24-36; D, $13-24; E, $7-13; F, up to $7. Plus 13% tax.

ple per cabina. Chinese manager helpful. Adjacent to national park at end of road.

Hotel Manuel Antonio: Pleasant, airy rooms. Upstairs balcony and lounge, not deluxe but nice use of wood. At end of road next to park, so handy to better swimming beaches. Food somewhat greasy.

Cabinas Ramirez: Better known as Mar y Sombra in past. Pleasant, ground-level rooms, some on beach, some in building behind. Price higher with fans; most people will need.

Bungalows: Bamboo huts in front of Cabinas Ramirez on beach with 2 bunks. Small, very basic shelter with showers, etc. in separate building. About $.80/day.

Playa Dominical

This beach area south of Quepos wasn't inspected this time, 36 km. west of San Isidro. **Cabinas Punta Dominical** advertises in tourist guides, with bar, restaurant, fishing, horseback riding. Apdo 196, San Isidro General, Puntarenas. Phone 25-53-28. There may be other basic or tourist accommodations here, but available information isn't up to date.

Golfito

Golfito I think has been badly underrated by others as simply a hot sticky banana port. It's a small town on the narrow strip several miles long, between a jungle-covered cliff and the Golfo Dulce, across from the Osa Peninsula. Near banana docks at the north end of town, the flat area widens out into the landscaped banana company housing, a mangrove lagoon, and the airport and golf course. Birdwatching in and around town is excellent. You can walk up a road on top of the ridge. Most hotels can arrange boats, fishing, snorkling, or visits to nearby fincas with wildlife. As the banana company land is converted to palm plantations requiring less labor, unemployment has risen and many people are struggling. Some North Americans live in the area, owning hotels and fincas.

Children walk Golfito's banana train track leading to the freighter docks.

Roads are good to Golfito. It's a 7-hour bus ride over the scenic Talamanca Mountains on the Inter-American Highway or a half-hour flight on SANSA. An air taxi operates out of Golfito providing the shortest air charters into Corcovado National Park. A ferry runs from town to the Osa Peninsula at Puerto Jimenez, but getting to the park from there involves hitchhiking plus 2 days of hot humid hiking uphill or around the south end on beaches. (Chartered skiffs to the park running around the peninsula from the outside have to go over a river bar with doubtful safety.) While not a primary destination, if you have time, a 2- to 5-day trip here is fun and adds another dimension to what you'll see of Costa Rica. The climate is humid and you'll probably want a fan at night. There are comfortable but no deluxe hotels in town.

Where To Stay

Cabinas Playa Tortuga: Very pleasant shaded yard with orchids. Cabinas have small patio.

Cabinas Delfina: Two styles—basic rooms with partitions not all the way up, no bath. More modern rooms with bath (cold water), ones facing away from street quiet.

El Puente: Price higher with air conditioning or fan. On right side above central district. Room light with skylight. Upstairs lounge. North American owned. Can arrange surfing, nature trips, snorkeling. Can fill air tanks.

Golfito: On left halfway through town. Gov't. employees stay here. Waterfront rooms preferred. Restaurant manager speaks English. Can take guests to her small farm with capuchin monkeys, etc. Recommended.

Gran Hotel Miramar: Rates higher in rooms with hot water. Launch available to charter for touring, scuba, fishing. Laundry service. Tours to cacao finca with orchids. On waterfront with super view. Cater to visiting yachts & can arrange fuel, provide anchorage. Large rooms. North American owned.

In Golfito checkout times are before noon because no one has dryers and sheets are expensive, so they must be washed and have time to dry before the afternoon rain!

A brown pelican takes off from ferry dock near Puntarenas.

Northwest Region
(Nicoya Peninsula, Guanacaste, Monteverde)

This region has the majority of Costa Rica's beach resorts, several of its volcanoes, and the biological preserve of Monteverde. Access by air is to many small resort strips or the regional airport at Liberia. Ferries cross the Gulf of Nicoya from Puntarenas and shuttle many times a day across the head of the gulf near the mouth of the Tempisque River. The Inter-American Highway runs from San Jose down to the western coastal plain and northward through Liberia to the Nicaraguan border. A good two-lane road, mostly paved, leads from the Puntarenas ferry terminal through Jicaral, Nicoya, and Santa Cruz to Liberia. A bus meets the ferry and runs north, though one usually changes buses at Santa Cruz. Smaller roads, some of them 4-wheel-drive all year and some only during the wet season, run from these towns out to the coast. All-weather roads run with bus service to Playas Tamarindo and Coco. While there's daily bus service to Nosara and Sámara, it can be an adventure in the wet season. Some of these buses go to the coast and stay overnight, coming back the next day. Their main purpose is to let the

River estuaries like this one in Guanacaste are fine places to see birds, monkeys, and other wildlife.

162

coastal people come to town to shop. It's a fascinating area, and bus riding is one way to see it cheaply. Some resorts have transportation all the way from San Jose, while others will pick you up at the local airstrip or at the Liberia airport. If there are several of you, or you're going to be on the coast for some days, a taxi ride from Liberia or Santa Cruz may be quite reasonable.

Santa Cruz, Nicoya and Liberia have festivals, rodeos and bullfights that are worth a trip from San Jose or a day in town from the beach. Remember that in Costa Rican bullfights, the bull chases the people around and isn't killed. When festivals are happening, you'll need hotel reservations, and your best chance of getting them is in Liberia, where there are a number of large reasonably-priced hotels. At presstime no one has yet put a tour or car rental agency in Liberia, though it's centrally located for a wide range of interesting day trips to mountains, beaches, rodeos, and national parks.

ICT is promoting more road signs and paving to tourist areas, but particularly around Sámara, Garza, and Nosara; the dirt tracks are presently quite anonymous and easy to get lost on, especially after dark. Do fill a car with gas in the main towns as most of the beach resorts don't have service stations.

Practically every village in the country has basic rooms or basic hotels at rock-bottom prices, generally cleaner than you'd expect from the outside, but frequently at a lower level than you'll want unless you're on a bare survival budget. There are some of the "we'd rather sleep on the beach" sort, though few of those are listed here. I stayed in one at Nosara when daylight ran out and there was a closed hotel to inspect the next day. The room was clean, but I had to be careful not to trip over the black pig in the backyard en route to the privy in the dark! Costa Rica has hundreds of hotels far above that level, but it has the full range. On the coast you'll want a building carefully aligned with the prevailing breeze or a fan, often more comfortable than air conditioning, and considerably more common. Starting with the Puntarenas ferry at the southern end of the Nicoya Peninsula, we'll work our way generally north, covering Lake Arenal and Monteverde on the way back to San Jose. Remember the considerable low season discounts offered by most hotels.

Playa Oasis Pacifico: On your left as the ferry from Puntarenas nears the dock. Very attractive, landscaped grounds facing gravel beach with shells. Waterfront bar with music, dancing. Screened open-air dining room, thatched shelters with hammocks, large clean pool, wading pool, tennis. Adjacent woods for birdwatchers, horses, fishing.

Hacienda La Tambor: On beach on south coast of peninsula, reached by boat, dirt road, or by landing small plane on hotel's lawn. Good reputation for food, quiet get-away-from-it-all place, adjoining working cattle finca. Not inspected.

Guamále: In village of Jicaral, first village north of ferry. Not resort area, but you could need a night here to make ferry schedule. Clean, with cold water, and has small, clean tipico restaurant.

Old church in Nicoya.

Nicoya

Nicoya is a marketing center for the southern peninsula and has a colonial church downtown.

Where To Stay

Curime: The only resort level hotel in town is actually a set of cabinas for 4 on landscaped grounds outside of town—very well done. Each has 2 single and 1 double bed, sitting room, bar, refrigerator. $33 for each cabina. Large pool. TV.

Alí: Basic, but all have windows. Cold water, beds & plumbing worn.

Cabinas Bema: Good beds. Light. Excellent value.

Chorotega: Basic front rooms not all with windows or partitions to ceiling. Back rooms open to court, light and airy.

Jenny: Large open style. TV in rooms; cold water, but very good value.

Las Tinajas: Enclosed parking behind. Manager speaks no English but friendly.

A villager rides up the beach at Sámara.

Town: Nicoya Peninsula – NORTHWEST REGION

Hotel	Address	Telephone	No. of Rooms	w/Bath	In Town	Courtesy Transp.	Air Cond or Fan	Parking	Restaur't	Bar	Elevator	TV	On Waterfr't	Pool	English Spoken	Noise Level	Cleanli-ness	Price Range
Playa Oasis Pacifico	Playa Naranjo Apdo. 200 Puntarenas 5400	61-15-55	37	all		x	fans	x	x	x			x	x	x	exc.	exc.	C/D
Hacienda La Tambor	Tambor Apdo. 398, San Pedro de Mtes. de Oca San Jose	25-98-11						NOT INSPECTED								exc.		?
Guamale	Jicaral Puntarenas	61-24-44 ext. 121	14	6	x											very good	exc.	C
Curime	Apdo. 51 Nicoya	68-52-38	20	all	x		A/C	x	x	x		x		x	x	exc.	exc.	C
Ali	Nicoya	68-51-48	31	all	x		Fans	x	x							exc.	good	F
Cabinas Bemer	Nicoya	68-52-59	11	all	x		Fans	x	x	x						exc.	very good	F
Chorotega	Nicoya	68-52-45	22	9	x		Fans									very good	good	F
Jenny	Nicoya	68-50-50	24	all	x		A/C	x	x			x				exc.	very good	F
Las Tinajar	Nicoya	68-50-81	19	all	x		Fans	x	x	x						exc.	good	F
Cabinas at Sámara	Sámara		?													good	poor	F
Cabinas Punta Sámara	Sámara	68-00-22	45		x		fans	x	x	x			x		NOT INSPECTED			?F

166

Sámara, Garza, and Nosara

These are 3 beautiful, light sand beaches reached from Nicoya. The villages of Sámara and Garza are at the beaches, while Nosara is inland. All are rather basic coastal villages without a resort atmosphere, though near Nosara there's a real estate development with many retired North Americans. The beaches have gentle surf and headlands at the ends. Fishing and boating aren't immediately obvious here, though a Garza boatbuilder builds fishing boats beside the road. Sámara and Nosara have very basic accommodations in town, but all have some tourist facilities outside. If you're avoiding crowds during holidays and make reservations for the limited tourist rooms, or camp, these would be a good choice. There's daily bus service from Nicoya though the road may be impassable in rainy season. Don't count on being able to drive north from Nosara in the wet season even with 4-wheel drive. Ask the locals about road conditions.

Cabinas at Sámara: Basic cabinas to left of road as you drive into town where road ends at beach. Were dirty and owner not present when inspected. Not sure what their name was.

Cabinas Punta Sámara: No signs to these and I didn't find them, but try road to left, south, when you reach beach. Call before going and get there in daylight so you can go on to Garza or Nosara if necessary.

Villaggio La Guaria Morada: Deluxe cabinas and resort with swimming pool, horseback riding, deep-sea fishing, and snorkeling. Not inspected, was still under construction but opened in 1984.

Playa Nosara: Attractive cabinas on ridge overlooking beach. Rate for single and double is same (per cabina) Tennis. Fishing. Canadian manager.

Playa Junquillal

Surf was up at this beach when I inspected. Swimming would require caution for rips though long scenic beach would be good walking or riding. Locals catch big fish from rocks on point. Camping is OK on north part of beach and would be improved

Town — Nicoya Peninsula - NORTHWEST REGION

Hotel	Address	Telephone	No. of Rooms	w/Bath	In Town	Courtesy Transp.	Air Cond or Fan	Parking	Restaur't	Bar	Elevator	TV	On Waterfr't	Pool	English Spoken	Noise Level	Cleanliness	Price Range
Villaggio La Guaria Morada	Garza	33-24-76 22-40-73 Telex: 3185 Guione	30	all	x	NOT INSPECTED		x	x				x	x		exc.		B
Playa Nosara	Nosara Apdo. 53 Boca de Nosara	68-04-95	8	all	x		fans	x	x	x			x		x	exc.	exc.	B
Playa Junquillal																		
Autumalal	Apdo. 49, Santa Cruz	68-05-06	20	all			fans	x	x	x			x	x	x	exc.	exc.	C
Villa Serena	Apdo. 17, Santa Cruz	68-07-37 33-58-78	4	all			fans	x	x	x			x	x	x	exc.	exc.	C
Playa Junquillal	Apdo. 17, Santa Cruz	68-04-65	4	all			fans	x	x	x			x		x	exc.	very good	E
Playa Tamarindo																		
Tamarindo Diriá	Apdo. 21, Santa Cruz	68-04-74	56	all		x	A/C	x	x	x			x	x	x	exc.	exc.	B
Cabinas Zully Mar	Tamarindo	26-47-32	15	all			fans	x	x	x			x		?	exc.	exc.	F
Doly	Playa Tamarindo, Santa Cruz	68-01-46	12	6				x	x	x			x		?	exc.	very good	F
Playa Portrero																		
Playa Potrero	Apdo. 45, Santa Cruz	68-06-69	10	all			fans	x	x	x			x	x	x	exc.	exc.	D

Price ranges for single room: A, over $52; B, $36-52; C, $24-36; D, $13-24; E, $7-13; F...

with some shade. There are 2 deluxe hotels and one set of cabinas here, with no village actually at beach. Access is from Santa Cruz or by flying into strip at Playa Tamarindo to north. It's
hard to imagine this area crowded!

Hotel Autumalal: Open all year with high season Dec.–Mar.
Deluxe duplex cabinas, brick floors, good beds. Thatched roof
over dining room on terrace. Rate includes meals. Fishing, tennis, horses. Wild monkeys live nearby and are seen on the
grounds. Attractive, in trees at south end of beach.

Villa Serena: Price includes meals, horses, tennis and equipment. Adults only, popular as honeymoon spot. No snorkeling,
some body-surfing. Large rooms. Dining on balcony overlooking
beach and landscaped grounds. May not take singles during high
season Dec.–April with limited room. Recommends watching
villagers fish from rocks or boats—sometimes use horse to haul
fish ashore.

Hotel Playa Junquillal: Is actually 4 cabinas, U.S. owned, not
deluxe but comfortable. Rate doesn't include meals. Whole place
sometimes rented by groups. Roofed, open dining room. Campers can eat here when open, Dec. through April.

Shrimp trawler in Papagayo Gulf.

169

Playa Tamarindo is 1 of only 2 Guanacaste beaches easily reached at present by public bus and all-year roads from San Jose (the other is Playa Coco) with a full price range of accommodations. These beaches do have a resort atmosphere, food and drink stands, and sometimes crowds and litter. (Fortunately the price of imported bottles saves Costa Rica from broken glass, as the bottle being worth more than its contents usually means you have to drink it where you get it.) The swimming is

At Playa Tamarindo, Cabinas Zully Mar has room doors carved from tropical hardwood in legendary figures. Each is different.

excellent in front of both villages and there's good snorkeling within walking distance. Tamarindo is famous for deep-sea fishing for sailfish and marlin. Seafood is excellent in restaurants here. Besides bus and car, you can fly via SANSA Monday and Friday from San Jose to the Tamarindo strip.

Tamarindo Diria: Deluxe hotel very well done, no seasonal rates. Game room with pool table, foosball. 3rd floor has great ocean view. Landscaped, shaded terrace between pool and ocean. Suites, with sitting room, refrigerator, bar, double and 1 single bed.

Cabinas Zully Mar: Comfortable large rooms with tile floors. Less than 100 yds. to ocean, restaurant and bar nearby. Rooms have individually carved doors illustrating Costa Rican legends. Excellent value.

Doly: On beach and well-aligned for breeze without a/c. Has some new rooms with price not known when I inspected. Great view.

Playas Brasilito, Potrero, Pan de Azucar

North of Tamarindo, across lagoon and river mouth is Basilito, a small village back from the beautiful beach which would be some of the nicest beach camping anywhere. Some development is occurring at the north end of the curved beach. Flamingo, next to the north, is a point with small bay, marina, yachts and very expensive beach mansions on the point above. Some villas in this area are rented and you'll see ads in the *Tico Times*.

Playa Potrero is just to the north with a long sheltered beach and good swimming. Behind is a creek with woods and good bird and monkey watching.

Playa Potrero: Very attractive beach hotel with large rooms in local hardwoods. No single rates. Quiet hotel with helpful manager couple who can arrange horses, snorkeling, scuba rentals including tank refills, boats with gear, fishing for sailfish, marlin, tuna. Coral reefs outside bay reached by boat. Highly recommended.

Children play in the Hotel Diriá's swimming pool in Santa Cruz.

Maintenance crew working at rear of Hotel Diriá in Santa Cruz.

The Tortilla Factory in Santa Cruz. In this sooty sheet metal shed, a dozen women produce excellent, very inexpensive food.

Bread oven at the Tortilla Factory in Santa Cruz.

Town / Hotel	Address	Telephone	No. of Rooms	w/Bath	In Town	Courtesy Transp.	Air Cond or Fan	Parking	Restaur't	Bar	Elevator	TV	On Waterfr't	Pool	English Spoken	Noise Level	Cleanli-ness	Price Range
Nicoya Peninsula — NORTHWEST REGION																		
Playa Pan de Azucar																		
Pan de Azucar, Sugar Beach	Apdo. 66, Santa Cruz, Guanacaste	22-03-18	6	all				x	x	x			x		x	exc.	exc.	D
Santa Cruz																		
Diria	Apdo. 58, Santa Cruz	68-00-80	17	all	x		A/C	x	x	x				x	x	exc.	exc.	E
Sharatoga	Apdo. 33, Santa Cruz	68-02-28	39	all	x		A/C	x	x	x				x	?	exc.	very good	E
Pension Cruz	Santa Cruz	68-00-33	11	all	x				x	x						fair	poor	F
Pension Isabel	Santa Cruz	68-01-73	26	all	x		fans			x						good	very good	F
Ocotal																		
El Ocotal S.A.	Apdo. 1, Playa del Coco, Guanacaste	66-01-66, 67-02-30	12	all			A/C & fans		x	x		x	x	x	x	exc.	exc.	A
	Apdo. 1013 (Estudiantes) San Jose, Costa Rica	22-42-59, 23-94-83, Telex: 3032 Ocotal																
South of Playa Coco																		
Bahia Pez Vela	150 E. Ontario St. Chicago, IL 60611	312-787-3323, 800-621-8091	6	6			fans — NOT INSPECTED						x		x	exc.	exc.	A

Price ranges for single room: A, over $52; B, $36-52; C, $24-36; D, $13-24; E, $7-13; F, up to $7. Plus 13% tax.

Pan de Azucar (Sugar Beach): New hotel opened early 1984. Manager not present when I stopped, so rooms not inspected. Dining room on terrace overlooking beach, done with taste. Covered porch in front of cabinas.

Santa Cruz

If you've gotten to any of the beaches above, you've probably come through this marketing and cattle town before this—if not, the coastal roads and trails will fail you and you'll have to bounce back to the arterial two-lane highway near Santa Cruz to head out to the coast on another road. As roads are improved and bridges built, other beaches such as Playa Ostional north of Nosara (with huge turtle arribas) will be accessible. Santa Cruz is an attractive town with 2 good hotels and several very basic places. If you come for a festival or rodeo, make reservations here or in Liberia as all rooms will be full.

Santa Cruz has a restaurant serving such good cheap food for lunch that it is busy despite being a sooty sheet metal shed 3 stories high! A dozen women inside make excellent tipico food and breads of all kinds, for less than $1 for lunch. Costa Rican government employees stop off here and U.S. TV crews taken to the Tortilla Factory for lunch at the long tables have raved about both the food and the ethnic experience. You can ask anyone for directions, but it's only a couple of blocks from the main square on a back alley.

Diriá: Very attractive hotel with large clean pool. Landscaping, hanging plants. Best in Santa Cruz and good value.

Sharatoga: Cool, attractive with shaded center court.

Pension Cruz: Basic, dirty.

Pension Isabel: Basic, clean.

Playas Coco, Ocotal, Bahia Pez Vela

El Ocotal: Deluxe resort done in excellent taste. Rooms in duplex cabinas along steep drive (not for new hip replacements!) with great view. Dining room on hilltop with view in all direc-

El Ocotal, deluxe hotel overlooking the ocean, has cabinas for guests down steep hill along drive.

tions. Tennis, horses, snorkeling, boat rentals, fuel. Have 2 coves & marina. Deep sea fishing is serious sport here.

Bahia Pez Vela: Deluxe small fishing camp for up to 12 deep sea fishing enthusiasts. Under same ownership as Isla de Pesca on east side. Not inspected.

Cabinas Chale: Very attractive cabinas in quiet northeastern outskirts of town still have short walk to beach. Rate is per cabina, for 1 or 2. Private walled courts behind cabinas. Very good value. Recommended.

Cabinas Luna Tica: Rooms for 4 or 6, not properly aligned to catch breeze. Basic.

Cabinas Catarina: Entry clean. All cabins occupied so could not inspect. Often rented by month and full. Single less than $2 even high season. Bring own fan.

Hotel	Address	Telephone	No. of Rooms	w/Bath	In Town	Courtesy Transp.	Air Cond or Fan	Parking	Restaur't	Bar	Elevator	TV	On Waterfr't	Pool	English Spoken	Noise Level	Cleanliness	Price Range
Playa Coco																		
Cabinas Chale	Playa Coco	67-00-36	10	all	x		fans	x	x	x			x	under const.		exc.	exc.	E
Cabinas Luna Tica	Playa Coco, Guanacaste	67-01-27	20	all	x		A/C in 10	x	x	x			x			exc.	good	E
Cabinas Catarina	Playa Coco, Guanacaste	67-01-56	5	all									NOT INSPECTED					F
Cabinas El Coco	Apdo. 2 & 3 Playa Coco, Guanacaste	67-01-67	74	all	x		fans	x	x	x			x		x	very good	very good	F
Flor de Itabo	Playa Coco (on right before town)	67-02-92 23-81-95	13	all			A/C	x	x	x				x		exc.	?	?
Playa Hermosa																		
Playa Hermosa	Playa Hermosa Apdo. 112 Liberia, Guanacaste	67-01-36	20	all			fans	x	x	x			x		x	exc.	exc.	D
Condovac La Costa	Playa Hermosa Apdo. 135 Liberia, Guanacaste	67-02-11 67-02-67 67-02-83	101	all			A/C and fans	x	x	x			x	x	x	exc.	exc.	B/C
Playa Panama																		
Pension Los Bananos	Playa Panama Apdo. 137 Liberia, Guanacaste	66-03-66	3				A/C	x	x	x			NOT INSPECTED					D

Price ranges for single room: A, over $52; B, $36-52; C, $24-36; D, $13-24; E, $7-13; F, up to $7. Plus 13% tax.

Cabinas El Coco: Good value with rates varying according to season and whether they face sea. Front rooms facing sea are well worth it; ask for rooms at far end away from bar. Food good. Recommended.

Flor de Itabo: Opened in early 1984. Well-done with hardwoods, big bathrooms, pleasant rooms. Price not known at time of inspection. On north side of main road entering town about 1/2 mile from beach.

Playa Hermosa

Playa Hermosa is a fine curved beach several miles long just north of Playa del Coco, with good swimming, and deep sea fishing and water sports available. There are 2 widely differing hotels at opposite ends of the beach—you can definitely pick your style here.

Playa Hermosa: Small attractive hotel among the trees just behind the beach. Owned by former Oregon couple who say "We sell tranquillity." Does considerale repeat business. Guests can visit the other end of the beach for water sports or an evening out.

Condovac La Costa: Large group of condos with unoccupied rooms available for rent. Scuba, fishing, water skiing, horses, tennis, discotheque. Golf carts transport guests to rooms. Acres of concrete overlooking Pacific. Furnished in vinyl and formica.

Playa Panama

Beaches are increasingly sheltered by Punta Mala as you head north here so surf is gone and water calm. ICT has major plans in this area with the Papagayo Project to encourage tourist development and take advantage of maximum good weather. Due to cost, most results may be several years off. There's a basic shelter and pulpería where the road reaches the shore here, in an otherwise rural area.

Pension Los Bananos: Was not inspected as there weren't any clear signs amid the dirt roads. It's reported to be good and is probably jus north of the pulpería above the shore.

Giant guanacaste tree, for which the province was named, shades Las Espuelas Hotel in Liberia. The tree blooms bright yellow in March and April.

Liberia
(pop. 14,800)

Liberia is the provincial capital of Guanacaste, a clean, busy town on the Inter-American Highway at its junction with the road to Santa Cruz and Nicoya. As I previously mentioned, it has excellent, reasonably-priced hotels, mostly with large cool swimming pools you'll appreciate in the heat, and an amazing variety of interesting day trips available if you have transportation. Most can be reached by bus, but the round trip isn't practical in a day with current bus schedules. There are several buses daily between Liberia and San Jose. From Liberia you can drive to most northern Guanacaste beaches, Santa Rosa and Rincon de la Vieja National Parks, Lake Arenal and Arenal Volcano with moving lava flows, Barra Honda and Palo Verde National Parks, and festivals at Nicoya and Santa Cruz and return to Liberia at night. I've found Liberia a good overnight spot to rest and clean up between camping trips to parks and beaches.

El Sitio: Large attractive hotel with architecture, decoration and planting all in Guanacaste cattle country theme. Wheelchair ramp even for 3 steps from lobby to pool level. Rooms without a/c are oriented to breeze. Recommended. Low season rates and honeymoon discount.

Las Espuelas: Very attractive hotel with entrance shaded by huge guanacaste tree (blooms yellow in spring). Interior courts with ponds and pre-Columbian figures. Planted breezeways, hardwood furniture in Spanish colonial style. Season discount close to 50%. Conference room. Very helpful manager with some English. Highly recommended.

La Siesta: Small, modern, pleasant hotel with good beds downtown. Small clean pool. Manager helpful.

Motel Bramadero: Has 6 rooms with a/c, usually occupied. Pool has been empty the 2 years I stopped by. Restaurant reported good.

Nuevo Boyeros: Big clean 2-story hotel around court with large clean swimming pool and wading pool with cascade. Cool rooms with good beds. Small restaurant serves good food, super fruit refrescas. Popular with truckdrivers and government employees. Dance floor in front (on weekends, ask for rooms at back for quiet). At about $6/single, this may be the best value in Costa Rica! Highly recommended.

Motel El Delfin: (not to be confused with the beach hotel at Esterillos). Trailer park, 10 rooms, 3 cabinas, dance floor, pool. Not open when I stopped, not able to inspect. Appeared somewhat run down.

La Ronda: Named for round dining room on second floor with good breeze. Rooms big with tile floors. Pool small. Hot water. Government employees stay.

Liberia: Basic. Partitions part way up.

Oriental: Basic. Chinese operated. Rooms without a/c very hot.

Town Liberia - NORTHWEST REGION

Hotel	Address	Telephone	No. of Rooms	w/Bath	In Town	Courtesy Transp.	Air Cond or Fan	Parking	Restaur't	Bar	Elevator	TV	On Waterfr't	Pool	English Spoken	Noise Level	Cleanliness	Price Range
El Sitio	200 m W on road to Santa Cruz / Apdo. 143, Liberia	66-05-74 66-05-73	54	all			A/C in 36	x	x	x				x		exc.	exc.	D
Las Espuelas	S on Inter-American Hgwy. Apdo. 88 Liberia	66-01-44 Telex: 6502 CRSpur	36+ 3 suites				all		x	x					x	exc.	exc.	D
La Siesta	Apdo. 15 Liberia	66-06-78	25	all	x		all	x	x	x		x		x		exc.	exc.	E
Motel Bramadero	Apdo. 70 Liberia	66-03-71	21	all	x		A/C in 6	x	x	x				x		very good	very good	E
Boyeros	on Inter-American Hgwy. Apdo. 85 Liberia	65-09-95	62	all	x		A/C	x	x	x				x		exc.	exc.	F
Motel El Delfin	N on Inter-American Hgwy. Liberia	66-02-30 66-02-97	13	all				x	x	x				x		good	?	F
La Ronda	Apdo. 81 S on Inter-American Hgwy. Liberia	66-04-17	22				A/C	x	x	x				x		exc.	exc.	F
Liberia	Apdo.80 Liberia	66-01-61	33	7	x				x	x						varies	good	F
Oriental	Ave. 2/ Inter-Amer. Hgwy. Liberia	66-00-85	29	9	x		A/C in 6		x	x						varies	good	F

Price ranges for single room: A, over $52; B, $36-52; C, $24-36; D, $13-24; E, $7-13; F, up to $7. Plus 13% tax.

181

Tilarán

This small town is high on hills above Guanacaste plain, near Lake Arenal. It's clean, with a cool breeze, and has several restaurants with good tipico food. There are lodges on the far side of the lake which I didn't reach. The country around the lake is lovely rolling upland with dairy cattle, and the lake is famous for fishing. Afternoon breezes across the lake can be very strong. Boats and fishing can be arranged though Tilarán doesn't seem touristy and all I met spoke only Spanish.

Where To Stay

Cabinas El Sueño: Light, airy, small hotel with rooms arranged around central court with fountain on second floor. Hot water. Manager very pleasant. Recommended.

Cabinas Naralit: Small rooms on ground floor, but light, OK. Cold water. Swimming pool empty when inspected.

Hotel Grecia: Basic. Some windows face concrete wall 2 feet away. Rooms at back are lighter.

Cañas

Cañas, on the Inter-American Highway, marks the turnoff to Tilarán and Lake Arenal. While not as cool as Tilarán, it's a central spot for trips to Arenal and the nearest good base for birdwatching in Palo Verde National Park and the Gulf of Tempisque.

Hacienda La Pacifica: Highly recommended by friends, though I didn't inspect it. Older, hardwood cabinas. Wildlife on premises, in and out of cages. Swiss food. 5 km north of Cañas on highway.

Monteverde

Monteverde isn't a national park; it's a biological reserve administered by the Tropical Science Center in San Jose. However, for nature lovers it's a major destination, as anyone who watches international nature programs on TV knows.

Town: Tilarán — NORTHWEST REGION

Hotel	Address	Telephone	No. of Rooms	w/Bath	In Town	Courtesy Transp.	Air Cond or Fan	Parking	Restaur't	Bar	Elevator	TV	On Waterfr't	Pool	English Spoken	Noise Level	Cleanliness	Price Range
Cabinas El Sueño	Tilarán, Guanacaste	59-53-47	12	all	x			x	x	x						exc.	very good	F
Cabinas Naralit	Tilarán	59-50-36	11	all	x			x	x	x						exc.	exc.	F
Hotel Grecia	Tilarán	69-59-43	?	4	x			x	x							exc.	fair-good	F
Cañas																		
Hacienda Pacifica	Apdo. 8, Cañas, Guanacaste	69-00-50	14	all	x		fans	x	x / NOT INSPECTED	x					x	exc.		E
Monteverde																		
Montana Monteverde	Monteverde Apdo. 7, Plaza G. Viques, San Jose	61-18-46 / 33-33-90	12	all		Y			x	x					x	exc.	exc.	C
Quetzal	Monteverde Apdo. 10165 San Jose	61-19-29	8	1		Y		x	x						x	exc.	exc.	D
Flor y Mar	Monteverde Apdo. 10165 San Jose	61-18-87	4		x			x	x						x	very good	exc.	E
Pension Santa Elena	Santa Elena								NOT INSPECTED			NOT INSPECTED						F

Price ranges for single room: A, over $52; B, $36-52; C, $24-36; D, $13-24; E, $7-13; F, up to $7. Plus 13% tax.

A group of Quakers from the United States and other countries founded a colony, choosing Costa Rica for its peace and tolerance. Today they and their descendants raise dairy cattle and goats on the steep slopes above the village of Santa Elena. Their cooperative makes very fine cheeses sold locally and in San Jose. Artistic members paint Christmas cards, calendars, and other products. The colony is at the bottom edge of the cloud forest, far from tropical heat—and at the end of a long winding road up from the Inter-American Highway (bus daily from Puntarenas to Santa Elena, 2 p.m.).

The reserve, partially donated by the Quakers, covers the upper slopes of the continental divide and laps over to the upper slopes on the east side. It has definite wet and dry seasons, though the upper levels have fog or rain much of the year. Paths wind for miles through the reserve which you can enter for a small fee that helps pay maintenance. There's more here than you can see in a day, even if you rent a horse. Many rare species, including the quetzal and the golden toad, are here among the several forest zones. You can come on a nature tour or on your own. There are several hotels and pensions as well as rooms for rent by local people if you're staying longer and living simply. While there is camping allowed, you'd be damp and cold rather soon.

Light rain gear or Goretex, and polyester bunting clothes that dry quickly are welcome. You'll want an umbrella in your day pack, which should be waterproof if you're going to walk far. Hiking boots are a must though they can be light. You'll want lightweight field glasses and a bird book. You can get bird and animal checklists as well as trail maps here. You'll see more in less time with a guide on a nature tour, but quiet walking on your own is a memorable experience and the local people are friendly and helpful.

Where To Stay

Hotel de Montaña Monteverde: First class hotel with 12 modern rooms overlooking the Gulf of Nicoya in the distance. Excellent food. Box lunches, guides and rental horses available. Will pick up guests from bus in Santa Elena. Sometimes have car to San Jose for reasonable charge (3½-hour drive). Tours from San

Tiled veranda of Hotel de la Montaña at Monteverde overlooks peaceful hills and the Gulf of Nicoya.

Jose can include day on Calypso yacht in gulf. U.S. owned. Costa Rican manager speaks English. Highly recommended.

Pension Quetzal: Very attractive modern pension with pleasant rooms, beautiful wood. Often full. Biologists often stay here.

Pension Flor y Mar; Basic, but pleasant, friendly. Price includes 3 meals. Can get box lunch. Rooms have bunk beds for 3 or 4. Nearest to reserve, 1½ km. Camping area adjacent.

Taxi from Santa Elena to pensions is about $6 each way.

Pension Santa Elena: in village of Santa Elena, near bus, but miles from reserve. Basic, not inspected. Reported noisy on weekends.

These separate areas, the "everywhere else" after we've discussed the areas with major tourist attractions, are getting only brief mention in this first edition for several reasons. They are interesting and sometimes beautiful places, but they can't compete with the coasts or the Meseta Central for the first time visitor's limited time. Except for the Inter-American Highway running through the Valle General, roads are often poor or non-existent. Except for those in San Isidro General, hotels are basic, well below the level most foreign travelers want. Finally, the political and military situation in Nicaragua in late 1984 has led to tension along the northern border, especially in its long central section, which is rugged and not easily patrolled. I hope with everyone else that these conditions improve and our next edition can explore these areas in detail while encouraging personal driving to Costa Rica.

For our purpose, south central refers to the Talamanca Mountains south of Chirripó and the Valles de General and Coto Brus. From the east, you can ride buses from Puerto Limón to Bribri near the base of these mountains. From there into the Indian reserves or up into the mountains requires 4-wheel drive until roads run out entirely and you're on foot. Especially in wet season, even the locals have trouble getting around. Several thousand Indians, remnants of pre-Columbian tribes, live in reserves granted by the government on the eastern slopes of the Talamancas. These bound the national parks of Chirripó and La Amistad.

On the west side, the Valles de General and Coto Brus are a developing farming area with a variety of traditional and new crops. The Inter-American Highway drops (often suddenly in the wet season or during earthquakes!) from the mountains down to San Isidro, the largest town and governmental center. Accommodations here weren't inspected but are reported good to basic and reasonably priced.

From San Isidro you can take buses to Playa Dominical on the coast or up Chirripó National Park headquarters on the edge of San Gerardo de Rivas. The Inter-American highway continues down the valley, down the river to Palmar and on to the Pana-

Beehives at an apiary produce honey while the bees pollinate nearby crops.

manian border. Buses to the border are crowded in the weeks before Christmas as Costa Ricans ride down from San Jose to shop in stores just over the border. Near Palmar the basaltic spheres of all sizes carved by prehistoric peoples are found.

In this area Costa Ricans and foreigners are developing fincas usually well off the main road. If you make their acquaintance and can visit, you will see pioneer life in the modern tropics and possibly some wildlife.

To reach La Amistad National Park, from Ciudad Neily, near the border, you can take a bus to San Vito and then over a very rugged road 30 km. to Las Mellizas. You should discuss this with the park authorities in San Jose first as you need permission and should get advice on routes from Las Mellizas, as well as what to bring.

A branch road and the banana company railroad cut west around one more ridge to Golfito on the coast.

For our purpose, north central refers to the area east and north of the volcano chain including the Cordilleras de Guanacaste, Tilarán, and Central. It's a rolling to hilly area that flattens out to the Caribbean lowland on the east. Roads lead from the Meseta Central to this region via Sarchí to Ciudad Quesada and via Heredia to Puerto Viejo on the beautiful Sarapiqui River (there are lots of Puerto Viejos in Costa Rica!). There are buses to both towns. At Ciudad Quesada, the largest town for some distance in the region, a cooperative has recently opened a store selling local arts and crafts. The road to Puerto Viejo passes 2 of Costa Rica's finest waterfalls and offers a great view over the northern region.

NATIONAL PARKS

You've already heard of the significance of Costa Rica's park system. Here's a brief outline of the attractions of individual parks and how you can visit. If you're not on a guided tour and are going to see more than Irazú, Poás and Manuel Antonio, which are heavily used and organized to handle crowds, you need to stop in at Park Service headquarters, Ave. 9, Calle 17/19, San Jose. Tel. 23-23-98.

Permission is required to visit most other parks and all of the biological reserves, which are preserved in unaltered condition for research purposes. Park headquarters has a 24 hour radio net with the parks, often their only way of getting assistance in an emergency. At headquarters there are bilingual staff who can get you the latest info on roads and conditions in the park. Out at the parks Spanish may be the only language. Staff at the parks is so limited that they must know when to expect visitors and whether you will need food, camping areas or bunkrooms (if they have them), guides, information, or horses. This is your best chance to find out what to bring and what to expect.

The Park Service has a very useful guide to the parks with the significance of each and some of the facilities (though more have been added since). It has bus info for reaching the parks. You'll soon note that most of the buses getting closest to the remote parks go to villages that aren't on any map you can find and let you off 10 or 15 km. from the park entrance (not what you may be used to)! Maps and wildlife checklists may be bought at the CIDA office in the National Zoo in San Jose. In many cases the nearest food is sold 20 or more miles from the park. Topographic maps are available at bookstores or the National Geographic Institute near Plaza Viquez, east of the Pacific Railroad station.

Costa Rica's national parks need and depend on international support as they've only been established a few years and the country has been unable to build needed facilities or, more important, to buy all the private land within them—in some cases a large proportion of the park. In the United States you can make a tax deductible gift to the parks for this purpose through either The World Wildlife Fund, 1601 Connecticut Ave. W., Washington, DC 20009, or The Nature Conservancy International Program, 1785 Massachusetts Ave. N.W., Washington DC 20036. In Costa Rica you can make a nontax-deductible gift to The Fundacion de Parques Nacionales, Apdo 236, 1002 San Jose. Tel. 22-49-21. It's one use for the money you couldn't change back to dollars on leaving or as a meaningful gift you don't have to pack for nature-loving friends at home.

Dimensions of the parks are given in hectares, equal to 2.5 acres. Parks we haven't discussed in detail include:

Santa Rosa Park Mucielago Addition: 11,600 hectares, sea level to about 100 ft. Former lands of Nicaraguan dictator, Somoza, on south shore Bahia Santa Elena, not contiguous with remainder of park. White sand beaches, some an easy walk from roads leading into area, much dry forest wildlife. Dec. through April best months.

At Tortuguero a baby green turtle, last out of the hole, skirts obstacles its first trip to the sea.

189

Tortuguero: Note that government boat from Moin gives priority to locals needing transport, so room isn't always available to tourists.

Guayabo National Monument: 19 km. north of Turrialba on 4-wheel drive road. Archeological site still being explored for life from 1000 A.D. to 1400 A.D. plus great birdwatching. 3000-6000 ft. November through March are best.

Barra Honda: Caves and very dry lowland forest near Gulf of Tempsique. Water and hiking trails are only facilities nearer than town of Nicoya, 14 km.

Chirripó: Highest point in country, upper level is páramo, above timberline, but park has 7 forest life zones with habitat for variety of wildlife. Three shelters for camping.

Rincon de la Vieja: Hike to summit only advised during dry season. One shelter en route available. Bunkroom at park headquarters also, plus several lovely single campsites at lower elevations. Don't camp or even stand longer than you have to on tick-filled lawn in front of headquarters! Wildlife & volcanic features spectacular. Bus unpredictable.

Rodrigo Herrera carefully approaches a boiling mud-pot, one of "Las Pailas" (the kitchen stoves) at Rincon de la Vieja.

Park headquarters at Rincon de la Vieja is an old ranch house built before the park was established. It has a bunkroom which may be used by visitors.

Braulio Carillo: On route of road from San Jose to Guapiles, and will be accessible. Barely so now—follow park directions. Wildlife, several forest zones, orchids.

Cocos Island: 600 miles offshore with reputed vast pirate and Inca treasure never found. Occasional tours available. Otherwise reachable only by chartered boat. Some species of flora & fauna found only there.

La Amistad: Huge, straddling upper slopes of Talamanca Mountains, adjoining park on Panamanian side. More than doubled size of Costa Rican park system. Newest park, with no facilities, trails, or services.

What a lot to explore! The wilderness aspects of these parks and heavy growth in most places can give you a much greater respect for short distances! But there's so much to see and marvel at, even if you sit quietly in camp and wait to see what walks, crawls or flies past.

191

SOURCES OF INFORMATION

TOUR AGENCIES

EXCAI Tours
Calle 26/28, Paseo Colon
Edificio Doble L
Apdo. 7.347, 1000 San Jose
Phone 23-01-55, 33-66-44

Agencia Super Viajes Ltda.
Calle 1, Ave. ctl.
Apdo. 3.985, 1000 San Jose
Phone 21-62-30, 23-54-92

Blanco Travel Service, S.A.
Ave. ctl., Calle 7/9
Apdo. 4.559, 1000 San Jose
Phone 22-17-92, 22-85-92

Agencia de Viajes
Panamericana Ltda.
Calle 5/7, Ave. 1
Apdo. 4.016, 1000 San Jose
Phone 23-45-67

Agencia de Viajes ATA Ltda.
Calle 3, Ave. 5/7
Apdo. 273, 1000 San Jose
Phone 21-71-47, 21-70-85

Agencia de Viajes Turinsa,
S.A.
Calle 3/5, Ave. 3
Apdo. 5.786, 1000 San Jose
Phone 21-91-85, 22-81-59

Viajes Receptivos, S.A. VIRSA
Calle 3, Ave. 1/3
Apdo. 892, 1000 San Jose
Phone 33-33-66

Finca Ob-la-di, Ob-la-da
Villa Colón, Costa Rica
Phone 49-11-79
Horseback mountain tours

Travel Bureau
Calle 24, Ave. 3/5
Apdo., 1000 San Jose
Phone 21-60-61

Jorge Léon Castro e Hijos
Calle 21, Ave. 1
Apdo. 1.630, 1000 San Jose
Phone 25-21-80, 25-72-73

Swiss Travel Service, S.A.
Urbanizacion Monserrat
Apdo. 7-1970, 1000 San Jose
Phone 32-67-42, 32-53-62,
32-08-67

Excursiones Aguila Dorado,
S.A.
Calle 21/23, Ave. ctl.
Apdo. 2.657, San Jose
Phone 21-41-57, 23-23-97

Costa Rica Travel Advisors,
S.A.
Calle 9, Ave. 1
Apdo. 986, 1000 San Jose
Phone 23-43-31, 21-20-39

Agencia de Viajes Turicentro,
S.A.
Frente Automercado Los
Yoses
Apdo. 3.251, 1000 San Jose
Phone 25-88-23, 24-55-55

Tikal Express Ltda.
Calle 7/9, Ave. 2
Apdo. 6.398, 1000 San Jose
Phone 22-68-22

Panorama Tours, S.A.
Calle 9, Ave. ctl./1
Apdo. 7.323, 1000 San Jose
Phone 33-02-33

Agencia de Viajes Proturis
S.R.L.
Calle 26, Ave. ctl./2
Apdo. 5.631, 1000 San Jose
Phone 22-91-09, 22-72-30

Central American Tours CAT
Calle 5, Ave. 1/3
Apdo. 531, 1000 San Jose
Phone 23-08-50

Agencia de Viajes Exintur
Calle 1, Ave. 7
Apdo. 1000 San Jose
Phone 23-71-75, 23-72-08

Agencia de Viajes Turisol, S.A.
Calle 11/13, Ave. 1,
Puntarenas
Apdo. 111, 5.400 Puntarenas
Phone 61-12-12

Interviajes, S.A.
Calle 3, Ave. 4 Heredia
Apdo. 296, 3000 Heredia
Phone 38-12-12

Costa Rica Expeditions
Calle ctl., Ave. 3
Apdo. 6.941, 1000 San Jose
Phone 23-99-75, 23-99-76
Raft and nature tours

Fiesta Tours, S.A.
Ave. 1, Calle 5/7
Apdo. 8-4320, 1000 San Jose
Phone 23-34-33

Agencia de Viajes Miki, S.A.
Calle 20 sur, Paseo Colón
Apdo. 328, 1007 Centro Colón
Phone 33-06-13, 21-36-81

Agencia de Viajes Atlántico
1078 Ceitro Colón
Apdo.
Phone 32-27-32, 32-88-88

Agencia de Viajes Turistas,
S.A.
Calle 38, Ave. ctl./2
Apdo. 115, 1007 Centro Colón
Phone 22-76-18, 22-67-62

Agencia de Viajes Las Olas,
S.A.
Hotel Jacó Beach
Apdo. 962, 1000 San Jose
Phone 61-12-50, 32-48-11

Viatur, S.A.
Centro Comercial del Oeste,
Pavas
Apdo. 394, 1000 San Jose
Phone 32-49-49

T.A.M.
Calle 1, Ave. ctl./1
Apdo. 1.864, 1000 San Jose
Phone 23-51-11

Alfavia Ltda.
Phone 21-62-22

193

Typical Tours
Ave. 4, Calle 24/26
1000 San Jose
Phone 23-46-93

Calypso Tours
Apdo. 6941, 1000 San Jose
Phone 33-36-18
Boat tours in Gulf of Nicoya

Papagayo Excursions
Playa de Tamarindo
Carretera San Jose—
Santa Cruz
Santa Cruz, Tamarindo
Guanacaste, Costa Rica
Phone 68-06-52
nature tours in Tamarindo
Estuary

Rio Colorado Lodge
Apdo. 5094, 1000 San Jose
Phone 32-40-63, 32-86-10
(Lobby of Hotel Playboy)
Fishing, canales trips, bird
hunting

Transporte Herradura
Hotel Herradura
Apdo. 7-1880
Phone 39-00-33

Sertur S.A.
Phone 22-06-73

Tursa
Ave. ctl./1, Calle 1
Edificio Alde
Apdo. 322, 1005 B México
Phone 33-61-94

Receptur
Phone 33-56-28

Mercurio
Apdo. 6490, 1000 San Jose
Phone 33-55-01

H. y L. Ltda.
Phone 23-93-49

EMBASSIES & CONSULATES IN/NEAR SAN JOSE

Nation	Address	Telephone
Argentina	Ave. ctl., Calle 27	21-68-69
Austria	Calle 2, Ave. 2	23-28-22
Belgium	Los Yoses	25-62-55
Brazil	Calle 4, Ave. ctl.	33-15-44
Britain	Paseo Colón, Calle 38/40	21-55-66
Canada	Calle 3, Ave. ctl.	23-04-46
Colombia	Ave. 5, Calle 5	21-07-25
Chile	Bo Dent	24-42-43
China	Los Yoses	24-81-80
Ecuador	Calle 1, Ave. 5	23-62-81
El Salvador	Calle 5, Ave. ctl.	22-55-36
France	Carret Curridabat	25-07-33
Germany	Ave. 3, Calle 36	21-58-11
Greece	Guayabos	25-9413
Guatemala	Calle 24/28, Ave. 1	22-89-91
Holland	Calle 1, Ave. 2	22-73-55
Honduras	Calle 2, Ave. ctl./2	22-89-91
Italy	Calle 29, Ave. 8/10	25-20-87
Japan	Rohrmoser	32-12-55
Korea	Calle 2, Ave. 2	33-10-56
Mexico	Calle 5, Ave. 1/3	22-54-96
Nicaragua	Calle 25/27, Ave. ctl.	33-44-79
Panama	San Pedro	25-34-01
Peru	Calle 4, Ave. ctl.	22-56-44
Spain	Calle 30/32, Paseo Colón	22-19-33
Switzerland	Calle 5, Ave. 3/5	21-48-29
U.S.S.R.	Curridabat	25-57-80
U.S.A.	Ave. 3, Calle ctl.	33-11-55
Uruguay	Calle 2, Ave. 1	23-25-12
Venezuela	Los Yoses	25-88-10

Call or visit in the morning, as afternoon hours vary.

COSTA RICAN CONSULATES

CANADA

614 Centre A. Street N.W.
Calgary, Alberta

7 Lia Crescent Don Mills
Toronto, Ontario, Canada

1520 Alberni Street
Vancouver 5, B.C.

1155 Dorchester Blvd. W.
Suite 2902, Montreal
P.Q. Canada H3B 2L3
(514) 866-8159
(514) 866-0442

UNITED STATES—Consulates General

Jurisdiction	Address
Washington, D.C., Maryland, West Virginia, Virginia	2112 "S" Street N.W. Washington, D.C. 20008 (202) 234-2946
New York, Pennsylvania, Connecticut, Delaware, New Jersey	80 Wall Street, Suite 1117 New York, NY 10005 (212) 425-2620 (212) 425-2621
Masachusetts, Rhode Island, New Hampshire, Maine, Vermont	250 North Beacon St. Brightow, MA 02135 (617) 783-3608
California, Oregon, Washington, Montana, Colorado, Wyoming, Idaho, Nevada, Utah, Arizona, Alaska, Hawaii	1680 N. Vine Suite 507 Los Angeles, CA (210) 461-9534
Florida, Georgia, North and South Carolina	28 W. Flagler St., Suite 806 Miami, FL 33130 (305) 377-4242 (305) 377-4243

Louisiana, Alabama, Mississippi, Tennessee, Kentucky, Arkansas	934 International Trade Mart New Orleans, LA 70130 (504) 525-5445
Texas, Oklahoma, Kansas, New Mexico	11570 Cheswood Houston, TX 77072 (713) 332-5052
Illinois, Michigan, Ohio, Indiana, Wisconsin, Minnesota, Missouri, North Dakota, South Dakota, Nebraska, Iowa	150 E. Ontario Street Chicago, IL 60611 (312) 787-3323
Puerto Rico	Calle 32 N 327 Avenida Américo Miranda Jardines Metropolitanos, Río Piedras Puerto Rico, 00927

There are many local consulates in each area. For addresses contact the Consulate General for your jurisdiction.

RECOMMENDED READING

Guidebooks, International, with Costa Rica sections:

South America on a Shoestring, by Geoff Crowther, Lonely Planet Publications, Australia. Lists hotels up to $7.00 per night. Much bus and transportation information.

The 1984 South American Handbook, Trade & Travel Publications Ltd., England (distributed in the U.S. by Rand McNally). Most information for the budget traveler.

Guidebooks, Costa Rica:

The Key to Costa Rica, by Jean Wallace, Editorial Texto Ltda., Costa Rica. Guidebook which emphasizes living in Costa Rica.

Costa Rican Life:

The Costa Ricans, by Richard, Karen, and Mavis Biesanz, Prentice-Hall. Very well done social history of the Costa Rican people. Up-to-date.

"What Happen"—a Folk History of Costa Rica's Talamanca Coast, by Paula Palmer, Ecodesarrollos, Costa Rica. Oral history by black coastal residents.

Natural Science:

A Field Guide to Mexican Birds and Adjacent Central America, by Roger Tory Peterson, Houghton-Mifflin. (Worth picking up before you leave the U.S.—it costs twice as much in Costa Rica.)

A Guide to the Birds of Panama, by Robert Ridgely, Princeton University Press.

Costa Rica: Country Environmental Profile—a Field Study, available in bookstores or at the Tropical Science Center, San Jose. Excellent in-depth study of environmental issues in Costa Rica.

Costa Rican Natural History, edited by Daniel H. Janzen, University of Chicago Press. Thorough discussion of the geography, climate, flora, and fauna of Costa Rica.

The National Parks of Costa Rica, by Mario Boza and Rolando Mendoza, INCAFO, Spain. Study of Costa Rica's national parks with beautiful photographs.

USEFUL ADDRESSES

The Tico Times
P.O. Box 4632
San Jose, Costa Rica
(located: Ave. 6, Calle 13)
Phone 22-89-52, 22-00-44

ASCONA
Apdo. 83790
1000 San Jose
Costa Rica
Phone 33-31-88
(conservation association)

TICA Bus
Calle 9, Ave. 4.
San Jose
Tel: 21-89-54

Language Institutes:

INTENSA
Apdo. 8110
San Jose
Tel. 25-60-09
    24 63-53

Instituto De Idiomas
Apdo. 741, Paseo de los
  Estudiantes
San Jose, Costa Rica
Tel. 23-96-62
Can arrange homestays.

Instituto Idioma Internacional
Apdo. 6945
San Jose
Tel. 25-31-55   25-01-35
     25-16-49   25-92-36

National Park Service
Ave. 9, Calle 17/19
San Jose, Costa Rica
Phone 33-52-84, 33-56-73

The Fundacion de Parques Nacionales
Apdo. 236
1002 San Jose, Costa Rica
Phone 22-49-21, 23-84-37

Tropical Science Center
Calle 1, Ave. 2
(2 blocks south of the Metropolitan Cathedral)
San Jose, Costa Rica
Phone 22-62-41

World Wildlife Fund
1601 Connecticut Ave.
Washington, D.C. 20009
(202) 387-0800

The Nature Conservancy
International Program
1785 Massachusetts Ave. N.W.
Washington, D.C. 20036
(703) 841-5300

Instituto Costarricense de Turismo
Apdo. 777
San Jose, Costa Rica
Phone 23-17-33

Costa Rican Tourist Board
200 S.E. First Street, Suite 400
Miami, FL 33131
(305) 358-2150 or 800-327-7033

ICT Office of Tourist Information
Plaza de la Cultura
Calle 5, Ave. ctl./2
Open Monday through Saturday,
8:00 a.m. to 7:00 p.m.

USEFUL WORDS AND PHRASES

abanico—fan
abierto—open
agua—water
alto—stop
Apartado (Apdo.)—post office
  box
apartotel—apartment hotel
aire (con, sin)—air
  conditioning
aquí—here

baño (con, sin)—bath
bolsa—bag
buenos días—hello
cabina—cabin
calle—street
cambio—change (money)
casado—basic meal
cerrado—closed
claro—light
comer—eat
comida—meal
comprar—to buy
correo—post office
cuarto—room
cuarto silencio—quiet room
cuenta—restaurant or hotel
  check

derecha—right
deseo—I want

lado—side
limpio—clean
lluvia—rain

médico—doctor
mercado—market
muy—very

nord—north

oeste—west
oscuro—dark

paraguas—umbrella
pension—inexpensive hotel,
  but does *not* indicate that
  meals are served
piscina—pool
playa—beach
poco—little
pollo—chicken
por favor—please
pulpería—small grocery store

que—what, who
quiere usted—you want (que
  quiere usted?—what do you
  want?)
quiero—I want

recto—straight ahead

dolor—pain
dónde está—where is

entrada—entrance
escuela—school
estacion, no estacion—parking
estampillas—stamps
este—east
farmacia—drug store
finca—ranch

gracias—thank you
grande—big

hasta luego (adiós)—goodbye
hay, no hay—there is, there
  isn't
hoy—today

iglesia—church
impuesta—tax (e.g., on hotel
  bills)
izquierda—left

salida—exit
semana—week
sucio—dirty
sud—south

tarde—late
temprano—early
tico (tica, female)—Costa
  Rican term for themselves
tiene—you, he, she, have or
  has
tipico—typical

ventana—window

Habla usted más despacio, por
  favor—please speak more
  slowly.

Numbers:

uno—1	diez y ocho—18	seiscientos—600
dos—2	diez y nueve—19	setecientos—700
tres—3	veinte—20	ochocientos—800
cuatro—4	veintiuno—21	novecientos—900
cinco—5	veintidos—22	mil—1000
seis—6	treinta—30	dos mil—2000
siete—7	cuarenta—40	
ocho—8	cincuenta—50	
nueve—9	sesenta—60	
diez—10	setenta—70	
once—11	ochenta—80	
doce—12	noventa—90	
trece—13	cien—100	
quatorce—14	doscientos—200	
quince—15	trescientos—300	
diez y seis—16	cuatrocientos—400	
diez y siete—17	quinientos—500	

FLASH!

As we go to press in December 1984, here's the latest news. The exchange rate is 48 colones/US $1 and some people expect that to increase.

Under the new head of ICT, Roberto Lobo, facilities and policies for the tourist are improving. The private sector is involved, and President Monge has declared tourism a priority of the government. There's a drive to cut red tape and airport taxes and pressure to reduce air fares to San José. Hotels on the coasts are being offered tax incentives to reduce prices, possibly by as much as 40%. Sr. Lobo is pressing for improved roads and signing to tourist attractions.

Some hotels are expanding and adding facilities, notably the **Cariari** and **Heradura** near San José. The tourist train to Limón with renovated cars, partly financed by tour companies, is available for a faster, more comfortable ride several days a week. The tour agents who contributed have a priority in bookings, so you may need to check with them (e.g. **Swiss Travel**). Tours and transportation on the Tortuguero Canals are being studied and will expand.

Life and costs for pensionados should improve soon. Roberto Lobo and Edwin Salas of ICT have campaigned hard with the legislature to remove recently added taxes, and that is expected to happen in January 1985. The same law will probably raise the required outside income to qualify for pensionado status to about $600 per month, but inflation had made the former $300 requirement unrealistic anyway for comfortable living.

ICT is trying to establish a one-stop system for pensionado applicants in its office with representatives from Immigration and the other departments involved. Only those who've struggled with the current system (or lack of it) know what a godsend that will be if it happens. "You have to take that form back to Casa Amarilla (Costa Rica's State Department). He stamped it, but he didn't initial it." Imagine having "him" at the next desk instead of blocks down the street with a 2-hour line in front of him, closing time in an hour, and a holiday tomorrow!

A pensionado association has formed to represent pensionado and foreign resident interests, inform its members, and coordinate with the pensionado department of ICT. Its members would be very good people to meet with if you're thinking of moving to Costa Rica. ICT can give you phone numbers and current officers' names.

I would appreciate any comments or information you're willing to pass along after your trip. This book will be updated regularly and small useful tips can be added between editions when we reprint. Unfortunately, I don't have time to plan trips or answer questions—several thousand readers quickly outnumber me and the 24-hour day.

Costa Rica is a wonderful place with some of the world's finest people. I hope you'll come and explore it—and have as great a time in this peaceful, beautiful place as those of us who've been here!

Stone corral, 300 years old, at Santa Rosa. Note snubbing posts for tying lassoed horses.

The author, Ellen Searby.

THE AUTHOR

Ellen Searby has traveled in 38 countries and 47 of the 50 United States by jet, her personal 2-seat plane, car, bicycle, canoe, raft, and on foot. She graduated from Stanford with a B.A. in biology and went on to earn a Master's degree in geography. She now lives in Alaska and has worked on the Alaska state ferries since 1975, first as a Forest Service naturalist answering thousands of travelers' questions, and more recently as a, member of the ferry crew. She writes and publishes *The Inside Passage Traveler*, an annually updated guide to the Alaska ferry system and the towns and regions it serves.

When she traveled to Costa Rica on a much-needed vacation, people who saw her book persuaded her to write a book for people going there, clearly explaining the choices they would have in sights, activities and facilities. She returned to do the research, and the result is *The Costa Rica Traveler*.

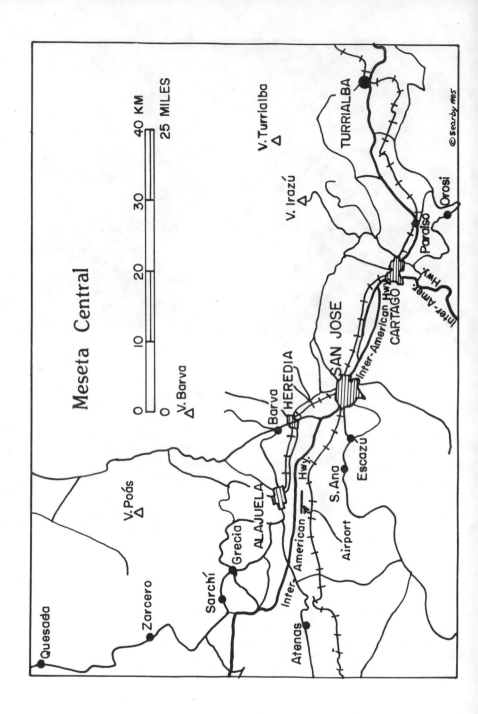

Meseta Central

V. Barva △

V.Poás △

Quesada

Zarcero

Sarchí

Grecia

ALAJUELA

Barva

HEREDIA

Atenas

Inter American Hwy.

S.Ana

Airport

Escazú

SAN JOSE

Inter-American Hwy.

CARTAGO

V. Irazú △

V.Turrialba △

TURRIALBA

Paraíso

Orosi

Inter-Amer. Hwy.

@ searby nes

0 10 20 30 40 KM

0 25 MILES

NOTES

Books from Windham Bay Press:
Box 1332, Juneau, Alaska 99802

The Inside Passage Traveler, Getting Around in Southeastern Alaska, 7th edition, by Ellen Searby. Photos, maps, 160 pages. Alaska! See more/spend less! Tells all you need to know to plan any kind of trip you want in the Inside Passage. This handy guide completely explains how to make the most of the Alaska ferry system, lists all the facilities in Southeast Alaska and Prince Rupert, B.C., with their prices, from deluxe hotels to cabins and youth hostels. Easy to read and use, with no paid advertising to weigh down your purse or pack. Enjoy a vacation according to your personal interests on this beautiful coast. $7.95 ppd surface, add $1 for air or $2 for foreign orders except Canada. ISBN 0-9605526-4-2.

The Costa Rica Traveler, Getting Around in Costa Rica, 1st edition, by Ellen Searby. Photos, maps, 208 (or more) pages. Enjoy this peaceful, tropical Camelot with its friendly people, miles of uncrowded beaches, tropical rain forest, volcanoes, and jungle waterways. Visit the country that has the most bird species (over 850) in the world, over 1200 species of orchids alone, altitudes from Atlantic and Pacific Oceans to over 12,000 feet, all in an area the size of West Virginia! Here is some of the world's best deep-sea fishing, snorkeling, river rafting—all at reasonable cost. Hotels, facilities and sights are clearly explained so you can make your choices. $9.95 ppd surface, add $1.50 for air or $2.50 for foreign orders except Canada. ISBN 0-9605526-5-0.

Windham Bay Press, Box 1332, Juneau, Alaska 99802

Quantity		Price*	Amount
_____	*The Inside Passage Traveler*	$7.95	_____
_____	*The Costa Rica Traveler*	9.95	_____
	Air or foreign postage:		
each	*Inside Passage Traveler*, $1 air, $2 foreign except Canada		_____
each	*Costa Rica Traveler*, $1.50 air, $2.50 foreign except Canada		_____
	Total in U.S. funds. Check okay if drawn on U.S. bank. No CODs or credit cards, please. Surface mail to East Coast from Alaska can take six weeks.		_____

Name _____

Address _____

City _____ State/**Prov.** _____ Zip _____

Country _____

*surface postage paid